Against Such Things
There Is No Law

The Fruit of the Spirit

Against Such Things
There Is No Law

Dr. Jaerock Lee

URIM
BOOKS

Against Such Things There Is No Law by Dr. Jaerock Lee
Published by Urim Books (Representative: Kyungtae Noh)
73, Yeouidaebang-ro 22-gil, Dongjak-gu, Seoul, Korea
www.urimbooks.com

Previously published in Korean in 2009 by Urim Books in Seoul, Korea

First Published in October 2013

Previously published in Korean in 2009 by Urim Books in Seoul, Korea

Edited by Dr. Geumsun Vin
Designed by Editorial Bureau of Urim Books
For more information contact at urimbook@hotmail.com

*"But the fruit of the Spirit is
love, joy, peace, patience, kindness,
goodness, faithfulness, gentleness, self-control;
against such things there is no law."*

Galatians 5:22-23

Foreword

Christians gain true freedom
as they bear the fruits of the Holy Spirit,
against which there is no law.

Everybody has to follow rules and regulations in their given circumstances. If they feel such laws are like shackles that bind them, they will feel burdened and painful. And just because they feel burdened if they pursue dissipation and disorder, it is not freedom. After they indulge themselves in such things, they will only be left with the feeling of vanity, and eventually only eternal death awaits them.

True freedom is to be set free from eternal death and from all tears, sorrow, and pain. It is also to control the original nature that gives us such things and to gain the power to subdue them. God of love does not want us to suffer in any way, and for this reason He recorded in the Bible the ways to enjoy eternal life and true freedom.

Criminals or those who violated the law of the country would be nervous if they see police officers. But those who abide by the law very well do not have to feel that way, but rather they can always ask the police for help, and they feel safer with the police.

In the same way, those who live in the truth do not fear

anything and they enjoy true freedom, because they understand that the law of God is the passageway for blessings. They can enjoy freedom like whales that swim around in the ocean and eagles that fly in the sky.

The law of God can largely be categorized into four things. It tells us to do, not do, keep, and cast away certain things. As the days go by, the world is increasingly stained with sins and evil, and for this reason increasingly more people feel burdensome about the law of God and do not keep it. The people of Israel during the Old Testament era suffered greatly when they did not keep the Law of Moses.

So, God sent Jesus to this earth and set everyone free from the curse of the Law. The sinless Jesus died on the cross, and anyone who believes in Him can be saved through faith. When people receive the gift of the Holy Spirit by accepting Jesus Christ, they become children of God, and they can also bear the fruits of the Holy Spirit with the guidance of the Holy Spirit.

Against Such Things There Is No Law

When the Holy Spirit comes into our heart, He helps us understand the deep things of God and live by God's Word. For example, when there is somebody we cannot really forgive, He reminds us of the forgiveness and love of the Lord and helps us forgive that person. Then, we can quickly cast away evil from our heart and replace it with goodness and love. In this way, as we bear the fruits of the Holy Spirit through the guidance of the Holy Spirit, we will not only enjoy freedom in the truth but also receive overflowing love and blessings of God.

Through the fruit of the Spirit, we can check ourselves as to how sanctified we are and how close we can get to the throne of God, and as to how much we have cultivated the heart of the Lord who is our bridegroom. The more fruit of the Spirit we bear, the brighter and the more beautiful heavenly dwelling place we will enter. In order to get to New Jerusalem in Heaven, we must bear all the fruits fully and beautifully, and not just some of the fruits.

This work *Against Such Things There Is No Law* lets you

easily understand the spiritual meanings of the nine fruits of the Holy Spirit along with specific examples. Together with Spiritual Love in 1 Corinthians 13, and the Beatitudes in Matthew 5, the fruits of the Holy Spirit are a signpost that guides us to proper faith. They will lead us until we reach the final destination of our faith, New Jerusalem.

I give thanks to Geumsun Vin, the director of the editorial bureau and the staff, and I pray in the name of the Lord that you will quickly bear the nine fruits of the Holy Spirit through this book, so that you can enjoy true freedom and become residents of New Jerusalem.

Jaerock Lee

A signpost on our journey of faith to New Jerusalem in Heaven

Everyone is busy in this modern world. They work and toil to possess and enjoy many things. And yet some people still have some life-goals of their own despite the trend of the world, but even these people from time to time might wonder whether they are really living a proper life. Then they might look back on their lives at that point. In our journey of faith, too, we can have a fast growth and take the shortcut to the kingdom of heaven when we check ourselves with the Word of God.

Chapter 1, 'To bear the fruit of the Spirit', explains about the Holy Spirit who revives the dead spirit, which became dead due to Adam's sin. It tells us that we can abundantly bear the fruits of the Holy Spirit when we follow the desires of the Holy Spirit.

Chapter 2 'Love' tells us what the first fruit of the Spirit, 'love' is about. It also shows some corrupted forms of love since Adam's fall, and gives us the ways to cultivate love which is pleasing to God.

Chapter 3, 'Joy' says that joy is the main standard with which we can check whether our faith is a proper one and explains the reason why we have lost the joy of first love. It informs us of the three ways to bear the fruit of joy, with which we can rejoice and be glad in any kind of circumstances and situations.

Chapter 4 'Peace' states that it is important to break down walls of sins to have peace with God, and that we have to maintain peace with ourselves as well as everyone. It also lets us understand the importance of speaking words of goodness and thinking from other people's viewpoint in the process of making peace.

Chapter 5 'Patience' explains true patience is not just to press down hard feelings but to be patient with a good heart that is free of evil, and that we will get great blessings when we have true peace. It also delves into three kinds of patience: patience to change one's heart; patience with people; patience with regard to God.

Chapter 6 'Kindness' teaches us what kind of person has kindness with the example of the Lord. Looking into the characteristics of kindness, it also tells us the differences from 'love'. Finally, it shows us a way to receive God's love and blessings.

Chapter 7 'Goodness' tells us about the heart of goodness with the example of the Lord who did not quarrel or cry out; nor break a battered reed nor put out a smoldering wick. It also differentiates goodness from other fruits so that we can bear the fruit of goodness and give out the fragrance of the Christ.

Chapter 8 'Faithfulness' teaches us about the kind of blessings we receive when we are faithful in all God's household. With the examples of Moses and Joseph, it lets us understand what kind of person has borne the fruit of faithfulness.

Chapter 9 'Gentleness' explains the meaning of gentleness in the sight of God and describes the characteristics of those who bear the fruit of gentleness. It gives us the illustration of the four kinds of fields as to what we should do to bear the fruit of gentleness. It finally tells us about the blessings for the gentle.

Chapter 10 'Self-control' demonstrates the reason why self-control is named as the last fruit among the nine fruits of the Holy Spirit as well as the importance of self-control. The fruit of self-control is an indispensable thing, which exercises control over all the other eight fruits of the Holy Spirit.

Chapter 11, 'Against such things there is no law' is the conclusion of this book, which helps us understand the importance of following the Holy Spirit, and wishes that all the readers will quickly become men of whole spirit by the help of the Holy Spirit.

We cannot say we have great faith just because we have been believers for a long period of time or just because we have extensive knowledge of the Bible. The measure of faith is discerned by the extent to which we have changed our hearts into heart of truth and how much we have cultivated the heart of the Lord.

I hope all the readers will be able to check their faith and abundantly bear the nine fruits of the Holy Spirit by the guidance of the Holy Spirit.

Geumsun Vin,
Director of Editorial Bureau

Introduction

CONTENTS

Against Such Things There Is No Law

Galatians 5:16-21

"But I say, walk by the Spirit,

and you will not carry out the desire of the flesh.

For the flesh sets its desire against the Spirit,

and the Spirit against the flesh; for these are

in opposition to one another,

so that you may not do the things that you please.

But if you are led by the Spirit, you are not under the Law.

Now the deeds of the flesh are evident,

which are: immorality, impurity, sensuality, idolatry,

sorcery, enmities, strife, jealousy, outbursts of anger, disputes,

dissensions, factions, envying, drunkenness, carousing,

and things like these, of which I forewarn you,

just as I have forewarned you, that those who practice

such things will not inherit the kingdom of God."

To bear the fruit of the Spirit

The Holy Spirit revives the dead spirit
To bear the fruit of the Spirit
Desires of the Holy Spirit and desires of the flesh
Let us not lose heart in doing good

To bear the fruit
of the Spirit

If drivers could drive down a clear highway they would have a feeling that is kind of refreshing. But if they are driving through that area for the first time, they would still have to take extra care and be on the alert. But what if they have the GPS navigation system in their car? They can have detailed road information and correct guidance, so they can reach their destination without getting lost.

Our journey of faith on our way to the kingdom of heaven is very similar. For those who believe in God and live by His Word, the Holy Spirit protects them and guides them in advance so that they can avoid many of the obstacles and hardships of life. The Holy Spirit guides us to the shortest and easiest way to our destination, the kingdom of heaven.

The Holy Spirit revives the dead spirit

The first man, Adam, was a living spirit when God formed him and breathed into his nostrils the breath of life. The 'breath of life' is the 'power contained in the original light' and it was passed down to Adam's decedents while they were living in the Garden of Eden.

However, when Adam and Eve committed the sin of disobedience and were driven out to this earth, things were no longer the same. God took away most of the breath of life from Adam and Eve and left only a trace of it, and this is the 'seed of life'. And this seed of life cannot be passed down from Adam and Eve to their children.

So, at the sixth month of the pregnancy, God puts the seed of

3

life in the spirit of the baby and plants it in the nucleus of a cell that is in heart, which is the central part of a human being. In the case of those who have not accepted Jesus Christ, the seed of life remains inactive just like a seed that is covered by a hard shell. We say that the spirit is dead while the seed of life is inactive. As long as the spirit remains dead, one cannot either gain eternal life or go to the heavenly kingdom.

Since Adam's fall, all human beings were destined to die. For them to gain eternal life again, they must be forgiven of their sins, which is the original cause of death, and their dead spirits must be revived. For this reason God of love sent His only begotten Son Jesus to this earth as the propitiation and opened the way of salvation. Namely, Jesus took all the sins of the entire mankind and died on the cross to revive our dead spirit. He became the way, the truth, and the life for all people to gain eternal life.

Therefore, when we accept Jesus Christ as our personal Savior, our sins are forgiven; we become God's children and receive the gift of the Holy Spirit. With the power of the Holy Spirit, the seed of life, which has remained dormant being covered by a hard shell, wakes up and becomes active. This is when the dead spirit is revived. About this John 3:6 says, *"...that which is born of the Spirit is spirit."* A seed that has sprouted can grow up only when it is supplied with water and sunshine. In the same way, the seed of life must be provided with spiritual water and light so that it can grow up after it sprouts. Namely, in order to make our spirit grow up, we have to learn the Word of God, which is spiritual water, and we have to act by the Word of God, which is spiritual light.

4

The Holy Spirit who has come into our hearts lets us know about sin, righteousness, and judgment. He helps us cast away sins and lawlessness and live in righteousness. He gives us power so that we can think, speak, and act in the truth. He also helps us to lead a life in faith having faith in and hope for the heavenly kingdom, so our spirit can grow up very well. Let me give you an illustration for a better understanding.

Suppose there was a child who was raised in a happy family. One day he went up to a mountain and looking at the scenery, he shouted, "Yahoo!" But then, somebody replied to him exactly in the same way saying, "Yahoo!" Surprised, the boy asks, "Who are you?" and the other one repeats after him. The boy got angry for that person was imitating him, and he said, "Are you trying to pick up a fight with me?" and the same words came back to him. He suddenly felt somebody was watching him and got scared.

He came from the mountain quickly and told his mom about it. He said, "Mom, there is a really bad guy in the mountains." But his mom said with a gentle smile, "I think that boy in the mountains is a good boy, and he can be your friend. Why don't you go back to the mountain again tomorrow and say you are sorry?" Next morning the boy went up to the top of the mountain again and shouted with a loud voice, "I am sorry for yesterday! Why don't you be my friend?" The same reply came back.

The mother let her young son realize what it was by himself. And the Holy Spirit helps us in our journey of faith like a gentle mother.

To bear the fruit of the Spirit

When a seed is sown, it sprouts, grows up, and blossoms, and after the blossom, there comes forth an outcome, which is the fruit. Similarly, when the seed of life in us which is planted by God buds through the Holy Spirit, it grows up and bears the fruits of the Holy Spirit. However, not everyone who has received the Holy Spirit bears the fruits of the Holy Spirit. We can bear the fruit of the Spirit only when we follow the guidance of the Holy Spirit.

The Holy Spirit can be likened to a power generator. Electricity will be generated when the generator runs. If this generator is connected to a light bulb and supplies the electricity, the bulb will shine the light. When there is a light, darkness goes away. In the same way, when the Holy Spirit works in us, darkness in us goes away because the light comes into our heart. Then, we can bear the fruits of the Holy Spirit.

By the way, there is one important thing here. For the bulb to shine the light, connecting it with the generator will not do anything. Somebody has to run the generator. God has given us the generator called the Holy Spirit, and it is us who have to run this generator, the Holy Spirit.

For us to run the generator of the Holy Spirit, we must be on the alert and pray fervently. We also have to obey the guidance of the Holy Spirit to follow the truth. When we follow the guidance and urging of the Holy Spirit, we say we are following the desires of the Holy Spirit. We will be full of the Holy Spirit when we diligently follow the desires of the Holy Spirit, and in doing so, our hearts will be changed with the truth. We will bear the fruits of the Holy Spirit as we get the fullness of the Holy Spirit.

When we cast away all sinful natures from our heart and cultivate a heart of spirit with the help of the Holy Spirit, the fruits of the Holy Spirit begin to show their forms. But just as the speeds of the ripening and sizes of the grapes in the same bunch are different, some fruits of the Holy Spirit can be fully ripe while other fruits of the Holy Spirit are not. One might have borne the fruit of love abundantly while his fruit of self-control is not ripe enough. Or, one's fruit of faithfulness is fully ripe while his fruit of gentleness is not.

Nevertheless, as time goes, each of the grapes would ripen completely, and the whole bunch will be full of big, dark violet grapes. Similarly, if we bear all the fruits of the Holy Spirit fully, it means we have become a man of whole spirit, whom God desires to gain very much. Such people will give out the fragrance of the Christ in every aspect of their lives. They will clearly hear the voice of the Holy Spirit and manifest the Holy Spirit's power to give glory to God. Since they completely resemble God, they will be given the qualifications to enter into New Jerusalem, where there is the throne of God.

Desires of the Holy Spirit and desires of the flesh

When we try to follow the desire of the Holy Spirit, there is another kind of desire that disturbs us. It is the desire of the flesh. The desires of the flesh follow the untruths, which are opposite of God's Word. They make us take such things as the lust of the flesh, the lust of the eyes, and the boastful pride of life. They also let us commit sins and practice unrighteousness and lawlessness.

Recently, a man came to me asking to pray for him that he would quit watching obscene materials. He said, when he first began to watch those things, it was not to enjoy them but to understand how such things affect people. But after he watched it once, he was constantly reminded of those scenes and he wanted to watch them again. But inside, the Holy Spirit was urging him not to, and he felt troubled.

In this case, his heart was agitated through the lust of the eyes, namely the things that he saw and heard through his eyes and ears. If we do not cut off this lust of the flesh but keep on accepting them, we will soon take untruthful things two, three, and four times, and the number will keep on increasing.

For this reason Galatians 5:16-18 says, *"But I say, walk by the Spirit, and you will not carry out the desire of the flesh. For the flesh sets its desire against the Spirit, and the Spirit against the flesh; for these are in opposition to one another, so that you may not do the things that you please. But if you are led by the Spirit, you are not under the Law."*

On the one hand, when we follow the desires of the Holy Spirit, we have peace in our heart and we will be glad because the Holy Spirit rejoices. On the other hand, if we follow the desires of the flesh, our hearts will be troubled because the Holy Spirit laments in us. Also, we will lose the fullness of the Spirit, so it becomes increasingly more difficult to follow the desires of the Holy Spirit.

Paul talked about this in Romans 7:22-24 saying, *"For I joyfully concur with the law of God in the inner man, but I see a different law in the members of my body, waging war against the law of my mind and making me a prisoner of the law of sin which is in my members. Wretched man that I am! Who will set me free from the body of this death?"* According to whether we follow the desires of the Holy Spirit or those of the flesh, we can become either children of God who are saved or children of the darkness who take the way of death.

Galatians 6:8 says, *"For the one who sows to his own flesh will from the flesh reap corruption, but the one who sows to the Spirit will from the Spirit reap eternal life."* If we follow the desires of the flesh, we will only be committing the works of the flesh, which are sins and lawlessness, and eventually we will not enter the kingdom of heaven (Galatians 5:19-21). But if we follow the desires of the Holy Spirit, we will bear the nine fruits of the Holy Spirit (Galatians 5:22-23).

Let us not lose heart in doing good

We bear the fruit of the Spirit and become true children of God to the extent that we act with faith, following the Holy Spirit. In men's heart, however, there are heart of truth and heart of untruth. The heart of truth leads us to follow the desires of the Holy Spirit and live by the Word of God. The heart of untruth makes us follow the desires of the flesh and live in darkness.

For example, keeping the Lord's Day holy is one of the Ten Commandments that God's children must abide by. But a believer

9

who is running a shop and has weak faith might have a conflict in his heart thinking that he will lose his profit when he closes his shop on Sundays. Here, the desires of the flesh would make him think, 'How about closing the shop every other week? Or, how about I attend Sunday morning service and my wife attends evening service to take shifts in the shop?' But the desires of the Holy Spirit would help him obey the Word of God by giving him an understanding like, "If I keep the Lord's Day holy, God will give me more profit than when I open the shop on Sundays."

The Holy Spirit helps our weakness and intercedes for us with groanings too deep for words (Romans 8:26). When we practice the truth following this help of the Holy Spirit, we will have peace in our heart, and our faith will grow up day after day.

The Word of God written in the Bible is the truth that never changes; it is the goodness itself. It gives eternal life to God's children, and it is the light that guides them to enjoy eternal happiness and joy. God's children who are guided by the Holy Spirit should crucify the flesh along with their passion and desires. They should also follow the desires of the Holy Spirit according to the Word of God and not lose heart in doing good.

Matthew 12:35 says, *"The good man brings out of his good treasure what is good; and the evil man brings out of his evil treasure what is evil."* So, we have to cast off evil from our heart by praying fervently and keep on storing up good works.

And Galatians 5:13-15 says, *"For you were called to freedom, brethren; only do not turn your freedom into an opportunity for the flesh, but through love serve one another. For the whole Law is fulfilled in one word, in the statement 'You shall love your neighbor as yourself.' But if you bite and devour one* another, take care that you are not consumed by one another," and Galatians 6:1-2 reads, *"Brethren, even if anyone is caught in any trespass, you who are spiritual, restore such a one in a spirit of gentleness; each one looking to yourself, so that you too will not be tempted. Bear one another's burdens, and thereby fulfill the law of Christ."*

When we follow such Words of God as above, we can bear the fruit of the Spirit abundantly and become men of sprit and whole spirit. Then, we will receive everything we ask in our prayer and enter into New Jerusalem in the eternal kingdom of heaven.

1 John 4:7-8

"Beloved, let us love one another,

for love is from God;

and everyone who loves is born of God and knows God.

The one who does not love does not know God,

for God is love."

Chapter 2

Love

The highest level of spiritual love
Fleshly love changes over time
Spiritual love gives one's own life
True love towards God
In order to bear the fruit of love

Love

Love is more powerful than people can imagine. With the power of love, we can save those who are otherwise forsaken by God and going the way of death. Love can give them new strength and encouragement. If we cover other people's faults with the power of love, amazing changes will take place and great blessings will be given, because God works amidst goodness, love, truth, and justice.

A certain sociology research team did a study on 200 students, who were in impoverished surroundings in the city of Baltimore. The team concluded that these students had little chance and little hope of success. But they did some follow-up research on the same students 25 years later, and the result was amazing. 176 out of the 200 became socially successful individuals as lawyers, medical doctors, preachers, or businessmen. Of course the researchers asked them how they were able to overcome such an unfavorable environment they had been in, and they all mentioned the name of a particular teacher. This teacher was asked how he could bring about such an amazing change and he said, "I just loved them, and they just knew it."

Now, what is love, the first fruit of the nine fruits of the Holy Spirit?

The highest level of spiritual love

Generally love can be categorized into fleshly love and spiritual love. Fleshly love seeks one's own benefit. It is meaningless love that will change with the passage of time.

Spiritual love, however, seeks the benefit of others and it never changes in any situation. 1 Corinthians 13 explains about this spiritual love in detail.

"Love is patient, love is kind and is not jealous; love does not brag and is not arrogant, does not act unbecomingly; it does not seek its own, is not provoked, does not take into account a wrong suffered, does not rejoice in unrighteousness, but rejoices with the truth; bears all things, believes all things, hopes all things, endures all things" (vv. 4-7).

How, then, are fruit of love in Galatians 5 and spiritual love in 1 Corinthians 13 different? The love as a fruit of the Holy Spirit includes sacrificial love with which one can give his own life. It is love that is at a level higher than the love in 1 Corinthians 13. It is the highest level of spiritual love.

If we bear the fruit of love and can sacrifice our lives for others, then we can love anything and anybody. God loved us with everything and the Lord loved us with all His life. If we have this love in us, we can sacrifice our lives for God, His kingdom, and His righteousness. Furthermore, because we love God, we can also have the highest level of love to give our lives not only for other brothers but also even for enemies who hate us.

1 John 4:20-21 says, *"If someone says, 'I love God,' and hates his brother, he is a liar; for the one who does not love his brother whom he has seen, cannot love God whom he has not seen. And this commandment we have from Him, that the one*

who loves God should love his brother also." Thus, if we love God, we will love everyone. If we say we love God while hating somebody, it is a lie.

Fleshly love changes over time

When God created the first man, Adam, God loved him with spiritual love. He made a beautiful garden toward the east, in Eden and let him live there with no lack of anything. God walked with him. God gave him not only the Garden of Eden, which was an excellent living place, but also the authority to subdue and rule over everything on this earth as well.

God gave Adam spiritual love overflowingly. But, Adam could not really feel God's love. Adam had never experienced hatred or fleshly love that changes, so he did not realize how precious God's love is. After a long, long time passed, Adam was tempted through the serpent and disobeyed the Word of God. He ate the fruit that God had forbidden (Genesis 2:17; 3:1-6).

As a result, sin came into Adam's heart, and he became a man of flesh who could not communicate with God any longer. God could not let him live in the Garden of Eden any more either, and he was driven out to this earth. While they were going through human cultivation (Genesis 3:23), all human beings, who are Adam's descendants, came to know and experience relativity by experiencing the opposite things of love known in Eden, such as hatred, envy, pains, sorrow, sickness and injury. In the meantime they became increasingly distanced from spiritual love. As their hearts corrupted into fleshly hearts due to sins their love became

17

fleshly love.

So much time has passed since Adam's fall, and today, it is even more difficult to find spiritual love in this world. People express their love in various ways, but their love is only fleshly love that changes over time. As time passes and situations and conditions change, they change their mind and betray their beloved ones following their own benefit. They also give only when others give first or when giving is beneficial for them. If you want to receive back as much as you have given, or if you get disappointed if others do not give you back what you want or expect, it is also fleshly love.

When a man and a woman date each other, they might say that they 'will love each other forever' and that they 'couldn't live without each other'. However, in many cases they change their minds after getting married. As time goes, they begin to see something that they don't like about their spouse. In the past, everything looked good and they tried to please the other person in all things, but they cannot do that anymore. They sulk or give a hard time to each other. They may get upset if their spouse does not do what they want. Just a couple of decades ago, divorce was a rare occurrence, but now divorce comes very easily and soon after divorce it seems that many re-marry somebody else. And yet, they say every time they love the other person truly. It is typical of fleshly love.

Love between parents and children is not much different. Of course, some parents would give even their lives for their children, but even if they do, it is not spiritual love if they give such love only to their own children. If we have spiritual love, we can give such love not just to our own children but to everybody. But as

18

the world becomes increasingly more evil, it is a rarity to find parents who can sacrifice their lives even for their own children. Many parents and children have enmity because of some monetary benefit or due to disagreements in opinions.

How about love among siblings or friends? Many brothers become like enemies if they get involved in some money matters. The same thing happens more often among friends. They love one another when things are good and when they agree on something. But their love can change any time if things become different. Also, in most cases, people want to receive back as much as they have given. When they are passionate, they might give without wanting anything in return. But as the passion cools down, they regret the fact that they gave but did not receive back anything. It means, after all, they wanted something in return. This kind of love is fleshly love.

Spiritual love gives one's own life

It is moving if somebody gives his own life for somebody else he loves. But, if we know that we are going to have to give our life for someone else it makes it difficult for us to love that person. In this way man's love is limited.

There was a king who had a lovely son. In his kingdom, there was a notorious murderer who was sentenced to death. The only way for that convict to live is for somebody innocent to die in his place. Here, can this king give up his innocent son to die for the murderer? Such a thing never happened in the entire course of human history. But God the Creator, who cannot be compared with any king of this earth, gave His only begotten Son for us. He loves us that much (Romans 5:8).

Due to Adam's sin, all mankind had to go the way of death to pay the wages of sin. To save mankind and lead them to Heaven, their problem of sin had to be resolved. In order to solve this problem of sin that stood between God and mankind, God sent His only begotten Son Jesus to pay the price for their sin.

Galatians 3:13 says, *"Cursed is everyone who hangs on a tree."* Jesus was hung on a wooden cross to set us free from the curse of the law that says, *"Wages of sin is death"* (Romans 6:23). Also, because there is no forgiveness without shedding of blood (Hebrews 9:22), He shed all His water and blood. Jesus received the punishments in our place, and anyone who believes in Him can be forgiven of his sins and gain eternal life.

God knew that sinners would persecute and mock, and eventually crucify Jesus, who is the Son of God. Nevertheless, in order to save the sinful human race that was destined to fall into eternal death, God sent Jesus to this earth.

1 John 4:9-10 says, *"By this the love of God was manifested in us, that God has sent His only begotten Son into the world so that we might live through Him. In this is love, not that we loved God, but that He loved us and sent His Son to be the propitiation for our sins."*

God confirmed His love towards us by giving His only begotten Son Jesus to be hung on the cross. Jesus showed His love by sacrificing Himself on the cross to redeem the mankind from their sins. This love of God, shown through giving His Son, is the eternally unchanging love that gives all one's life even to the last drop of blood.

True love towards God

Can we also possess such level of love? 1 John 4:7-8 says, *"Beloved, let us love one another, for love is from God; and everyone who loves is born of God and knows God. The one who does not love does not know God, for God is love."*

If we know not just as head knowledge, but deeply feel in our hearts the kind of love God has given to us, we will naturally love God truthfully. In our Christian lives, we might face trials that are difficult to bear, or we might encounter a situation where we can lose all our possessions and things precious to us. Even in those situations, our hearts will not be shaken at all as long as we have true love in us.

I almost lost all three of my precious daughters. More than 30 years ago in Korea, most people used coal briquettes for heating. The carbon monoxide gas from the coal often caused accidents. It was right after the opening of the church and my residence was in the basement of the church building. My three daughters, along with a young man, had carbon-monoxide gas-poisoning. They had inhaled the gas all night, and there seemed to be no hope of recovery.

Seeing my unconscious daughters, I did not have any sorrow or complaints. I was only thankful thinking they were going to live peacefully in the beautiful Heaven where there are no tears, sorrow, or pain. But because the young man was just a church member, I asked God to revive that man so as not to disgrace God. I laid my hands on the young man and prayed for him. And then, I prayed for my third and youngest daughter. While I was praying for her, the young man gained consciousness. While I was praying for the second daughter, the third one woke up. Soon, both my second and first daughter returned to consciousness. They did not suffer any after-effects, and up to this day they are healthy. All three of them are ministering as pastors in the church.

If we love God, our love will never change in any kind of situation. We have already received His love of sacrificing His only begotten Son, and therefore we do not have any reason to resent Him or doubt His love. We can only love Him unchangingly. We can only trust His love completely and be faithful to Him with our lives.

This attitude will not change when we take care of other souls, too. 1 John 3:16 says, *"We know love by this, that He laid down His life for us; and we ought to lay down our lives for the brethren."* If we cultivate true love toward God, we will love our brothers with true love. It means we will not have any desire to seek our own, and thus we will give everything we have and not want anything in return. We will sacrifice ourselves with pure motives and give all our possessions for others.

I have gone through numerous trials as I have been walking the way of faith up to this day. I was betrayed by those people who received so many things from me, or those whom I treated as my own family. Sometimes the people misunderstood me and pointed their fingers at me.

22

Nevertheless, I just treated them with goodness. I committed all matters into God's hands and prayed that He would forgive such people with His love and compassion. I did not hate even those people who caused great difficulties for the church and left. I just wanted them to repent and come back. When those people did many evil things, it caused intense trials for me. Nevertheless, I treated them only with goodness because I believed God loved me, and because I loved them with the love of God.

In order to bear the fruit of love

We can bear the fruit of love completely to the extent that we sanctify our hearts by casting away sins, evil, and lawlessness from our hearts. True love can come out from a heart that is free of evil. If we possess true love, we can give others peace all the time and would never give a hard time to or lay a burden on others. We would also understand others' hearts and serve them. We would be able to give them joy and help to allow their souls to prosper so that the kingdom of God could be extended.

In the Bible, we can see what kind of love the fathers of faith had cultivated. Moses loved his people, Israel, so very much that he wanted to save them even if it meant his name would be blotted out from the book of life (Exodus 32:32).

The apostle Paul also loved the Lord with an unchanging mind from the time he met Him. He became an apostle to the Gentiles, and saved many souls and established churches through his three mission trips. Though his way was exhausting and full of peril, he preached Jesus Christ until he was martyred in Rome.

There were constant life threats and persecutions and disturbance from the Jews. He was beaten and put in jail. He was adrift in the sea a night and a day after a shipwreck. Nevertheless, he never regretted the way he chose. Instead of concern for himself he was concerned about the church and the believers even while he was going through the many hardships.

He expressed his feelings in 2 Corinthians 11:28-29, which says, *"Apart from such external things, there is the daily pressure on me of concern for all the churches. Who is weak without my being weak? Who is led into sin without my intense concern?"*

The apostle Paul did not spare even his life because he had burning love for the souls. His great love is well-expressed in Romans 9:3. It says, *"For I could wish that I myself were accursed, separated from Christ for the sake of my brethren, my kinsmen according to the flesh."* Here, 'my kinsmen' does not mean family or relatives. It refers to all the Jews including those who were persecuting him.

He would rather go to Hell in their place, only if it could save those people. This is the kind of love he possessed. Also, as written in John 15:13, *"Greater love has no one than this, that one lay down his life for his friends,"* the apostle Paul proved his highest level of love by becoming a martyr.

Some people say they love the Lord but they do not love their brothers in faith. These brothers are not even their enemies nor are they asking for one's life. But they have conflicts with and harbor uncomfortable feelings against each other over trivial matters. Even while doing the work of God, they have hard feelings when their opinions are different. Some people are insensitive about other people whose spirits are withering and dying. Then, can we say such people love God?

Once I professed before the whole congregation. I said, "If I can save one thousand souls, I'd be willing to go to Hell in their place." Of course, I know what kind of place Hell is very well. I will never do anything that will make me go to Hell. But if I can save those souls who are falling into Hell, I'd be willing to go there in their place.

Those one thousand souls could include some of our church members. It could be church leaders or members who do not choose the truth but go the way of death even after hearing the words of truth and witnessing the powerful works of God. Also, they could be those people who persecute our church with their misunderstandings and jealousy. Or, they could be some poor souls in Africa who are starving due to civil wars, famine, and poverty.

Just as Jesus died for me, I can give my life for them, too. It is not because I love them as a part of my duty, just because God's Word says we have to love. I give all my life and energy day by day to save them, because I love them more than my life and not just with words. I give all my life because I know it is the greatest desire of the Father God who loved me.

My heart is full of such thoughts as, 'How can I preach the gospel in more places?' 'How can I manifest greater works of God's power so more people can believe?' 'How can I let them understand the meaninglessness of this world and lead them to

Love

take hold of the heavenly kingdom?'

Let us look back on ourselves as to how much love of God is engraved in us. It is the love with which He gave the life of His only begotten Son. If we are full of His love, we will love God and the souls with all our hearts. This is true love. And, if we cultivate this love completely, we will be able to enter into New Jerusalem, which is the crystalloid of love. I hope all of you will share eternal love with the Father God and the Lord there.

Philippians 4:4

"Rejoice in the Lord always;

again I will say, rejoice!"

Chapter 3

Joy

Joy

Laughter alleviates stress, anger, and tension thereby contributing to the prevention of heart attack and sudden death. It also improves the immunity of the body, so it has positive effects in prevention of infections like flu or even such diseases as cancers and diseases attributed to lifestyle. Laughter certainly has very positive effects on our health, and God also tells us to rejoice always. Some might say, "How can I rejoice when there is nothing to rejoice about?" But, men of faith can always rejoice in the Lord because they believe God will help them out of hardships, and they will eventually be guided to the kingdom of heaven where there is eternal joy.

The fruit of joy

Joy is "intense and especially ecstatic or exultant happiness." Spiritual joy, however, is not just to be extremely happy. Even unbelievers rejoice when things are good, but this is only temporary. Their joy disappears when things become difficult. But if we bear the fruit of joy in our hearts we will be able to rejoice and be glad in any kind of situation.

1 Thessalonians 5:16-18 says, *"Rejoice always; pray without ceasing; in everything give thanks; for this is God's will for you in Christ Jesus."* Spiritual joy is to rejoice always and give thanks in all circumstances. Joy is one of the most obvious and clearest of the categories with which we can measure and check what kind of Christian life we are leading.

Some believers walk the way of the Lord with joy and happiness all the time while some others do not really have true joy and thanks stemming from their hearts, though they might be trying hard in their faith. They attend worship services, pray, and fulfill their church duties, but they do all these activities as if they were fulfilling a duty being unmoved. And if they encounter any problem, they lose the least bit of peace they had and their hearts are shaken by nervousness.

If there is a problem that you can never solve with your own strength, this is when you can check whether you are really rejoicing from the depth of your heart. In such a situation, why don't you look into a mirror? It can also become a measurement to check to what extent you have borne the fruit of joy. As a matter of fact, just the grace of Jesus Christ saving us through His blood is more than enough condition for us to rejoice all the time. We were destined to fall into eternal fire in Hell, but through the blood of Jesus Christ we were enabled to go into the kingdom of heaven filled with happiness and peace. This fact alone can give us happiness beyond words.

After the Exodus when the sons of Israel crossed the Red Sea as though on dry land and were set free from the Egyptian army that was chasing them, how greatly did they rejoice? Filled with happiness the women danced with timbrels and all the people praised God (Exodus 15:19-20).

Similarly, when one accepts the Lord, he has inexpressible joy over being saved, and he can always sing with praises on his lips even if he is tired after a day of hard labor. Even if he is persecuted for the name of the Lord or suffers a hardship without just cause, he is just happy thinking about the kingdom of heaven. If this joy is continually and fully maintained, he will soon bear the fruit of

Against Such Things There Is No Law

joy completely.

The reasons why the joy
of the first love disappears

In reality, however, not so many people keep the joy of their first love. Sometime after they accept the Lord, the joy disappears and their emotions with regard to the grace of salvation are no longer the same. In the past, they were just happy even in hardships thinking about the Lord, but later they begin to sigh and lament when things are hard. It is just like the sons of Israel who very quickly forgot the joy they had after crossing the Red Sea and complained against God and stood against Moses for little difficulties.

Why do people change this way? It is because they have flesh in their hearts. The flesh here has a spiritual meaning. It refers to the natures or characters that are opposite to spirit. 'Spirit' is something that belongs to God the Creator, which is beautiful and never-changing, while 'flesh' is the characteristics of the things that are severed from God. They are the things that will perish, corrupt, and disappear. Therefore, all kinds of sins such as lawlessness, unrighteousness, and untruths are flesh. Those who have such attributes of flesh will lose their joy which once fully filled their hearts. Also, because they have changing natures, the enemy devil and Satan try to cause situations to be unfavorable by agitating that changing nature.

The apostle Paul was beaten and put in prison while preaching the gospel. But as he prayed and praised God without worrying about anything, a great earthquake occurred and the prison doors were opened. Furthermore, through this event, he evangelized many unbelievers. He did not lose his joy in any hardship, and he advised the believers to *"Rejoice in the Lord always; again I will say, rejoice! Let your gentle spirit be known to all men. The Lord is near. Be anxious for nothing, but in everything by prayer and supplication with thanksgiving let your requests be made known to God"* (Philippians 4:4-6).

If you are in a dire situation as if you were clinging to the edge of a cliff, why don't you offer a prayer of thanksgiving like the apostle Paul? God will be pleased with your act of faith and He will work for the good in everything.

When spiritual joy is borne

David fought on the battlefields for his country from the time he was in his youth. He rendered meritorious services in many different wars. When King Saul was suffering from evil spirits, he played the harp to give peace to the king. He never violated an order from his king. Nevertheless, King Saul was not grateful for David's service, but in fact he hated David because he was jealous of him. Because David was loved by the people, Saul was afraid that his throne would be taken, and he pursued David with his army to kill him.

In such a situation, David obviously had to flee from Saul. Once, in order to save his life in a foreign country, he had to drool pretending to be mad. How would you feel if you were in his shoes? David was never saddened but he only rejoiced. He professed his faith in God with a beautiful psalm.

"The LORD is my shepherd, I shall not want.
He makes me lie down in green pastures;
He leads me beside quiet waters.
He restores my soul;
He guides me in the paths of righteousness
For His name's sake.
Even though I walk through
the valley of the shadow of death,
I fear no evil, for You are with me;
Your rod and Your staff, they comfort me.
You prepare a table before me
in the presence of my enemies;
You have anointed my head with oil; My cup overflows.
Surely goodness and lovingkindness will follow me
all the days of my life,
and I will dwell in the house of the LORD forever"
(Psalm 23:1-6).

The reality was like a road of thorns, but David had something great in him. It was his burning love toward and unchanging trust in God. Nothing could take away the joy stemming from the depth of his heart. David was certainly a person who had borne the fruit of joy.

For about forty-one years since I accepted the Lord, I have never lost the joy of my first love. I still live each day with gratefulness. I had suffered from so many diseases for seven years, but God's power healed all those illnesses at once. Immediately I became a Christian and began to work on construction sites. I had a chance to get a better job but I chose to do the hard labor because it was the only way for me to keep the Lord's Day holy.

Every morning I used to get up at four o'clock and attend the dawn prayer meetings. Then I went to work with a packed lunch. It took about an hour and a half by bus to get to the workplace. I had to work from morning till evening without getting enough rest. It was really hard labor. I had never done physical labor before and on top of that I had been sick for so many years, so it was not an easy job for me.

I would come back around ten o'clock at night, after work. I briefly washed up, had dinner, read the Bible and prayed before I went to sleep at around midnight. My wife was also doing door-to-door sales to earn a living, but it was difficult for us to pay back just the interest on the debt we had accumulated during the period I had been sick. Literally, we could barely make ends meet every day. Although I was in a very difficult situation financially, my heart was always filled with joy and I preached the gospel every time I had a chance.

I would say, "God is alive! Look at me! I was waiting only for death, but I was totally healed by God's power and I have become this healthy!"

The reality was difficult and financially challenging, but I was always thankful for the love of God who saved me from death. My heart was also filled with hope of Heaven. After I received the call of God to become a pastor, I suffered many unjust hardships and things that a man cannot really bear with, and yet my joy and gratefulness never cooled down.

How was it possible? It is because thankfulness of the heart gives birth to more thankfulness. I always look for the things to give thanks for and offer prayers of thanksgiving to God. And not only prayer of thanks, I enjoy giving thanksgiving offerings to God. In addition to the thanksgiving offerings I offered to God at every worship service, I diligently gave thanks offerings to God for other things. I gave thanks for the church members who are growing up in faith; for letting me give glory to God through mega-sized overseas crusades; for giving church growth, etc. I enjoy searching for the conditions of thanksgiving.

So, God gave me blessings and grace without ceasing so that I could only keep on giving thanks. If I had given thanks only when things were good and not given thanks but complained when things were bad, I wouldn't have had the happiness I enjoy now.

If you want to bear the fruit of joy

First, you should cast off flesh.

If we do not have envy or jealousy, we will rejoice when others are praised or blessed as if we were being praised and blessed. On the contrary, we will have a hard time watching others becoming well-off to the extent that we have envy and jealousy. We might have uncomfortable feelings about others, or we lose joy and become disheartened because we might feel inferior to the extent others are lifted up.

Also, if we do not have anger or resentment, we will have only peace even if we are treated rudely or sustain damage. We become resentful and disappointed because we have flesh in us. This flesh is the burden that makes us feel heavy-laden in heart. If we have the nature to seek our own benefit, we will feel very bad and painful when it seems that we are suffering a greater loss than others.

Because we have fleshly attributes in us, the enemy devil and Satan agitate these fleshly natures to create situations where we cannot rejoice. To the extent that we have flesh, we cannot have spiritual faith, and we will have increasingly more worries and concerns being unable to rely on God. But those who rely on God can rejoice even if they do not have anything to eat today. It is because God promised us that He would give us what we need when we seek first His kingdom and righteousness (Matthew 6:31-33).

Those who have true faith will commit every matter into God's hands through prayers of thanksgiving in any kind of hardship. They will seek God's kingdom and righteousness with a peaceful heart and then ask for what they need. But those who do not rely on God but on their own thoughts and plans cannot help but become restless. Those who do businesses can be led to the prosperous ways and receive blessings only if they can hear the voice of the Holy Spirit clearly and follow it. But as long as they have greed, impatience, and thoughts of untruths, they cannot hear the voice of the Holy Spirit and they will face difficulties. In summation, the fundamental reason why we lose joy is the fleshly attributes that we have in our heart. We will have increasingly more spiritual joy and thanks, and all things will go well with us to the extent that we cast off flesh from our heart.

38

Second, we have to follow the desires of the Holy Spirit in all things.

The joy we seek is not worldly joy but the joy that comes from above, namely the joy of the Holy Spirit. We can be joyful and happy only when the Holy Spirit dwelling in us rejoices. Above all, true joy comes when we worship God with our heart, pray to and praise Him, and keep His Word.

Also, if we realize our shortcomings through the inspiration of the Holy Spirit and improve them, how happy we become! We are more apt to be happy and grateful when we find our new 'self' who is different from who we were before. The joy given by God cannot be compared with any joy of the world, and nobody can take it away.

Depending on what kinds of choices we make in our daily lives, we might follow the desires of the Holy Spirit or those of the flesh. If we follow the desires of the Holy Spirit every moment, the Holy Spirit rejoices in us and fills us with joy. 3 John 1:4 says, *"I have no greater joy than this, to hear of my children walking in the truth."* As said, God rejoices and gives us joy in the fullness of the Holy Spirit when we practice the truth.

For example, if the desire to seek our own benefit and the desire to seek others' benefit collide with each other, and if this conflict goes on, we will lose joy. Then, if we eventually seek our own benefit, it seems that we can take what we wanted, but we will not gain spiritual joy. But rather, we will have pangs of conscience or afflictions in heart. On the other course, if we seek others' benefit, it might seem that we are suffering a loss for the moment, but we will gain joy from above because the Holy Spirit rejoices. Only those who have actually felt such joy will understand how good it is. It is the kind of happiness that nobody in the world can give or understand.

There is a story of two brothers. The elder one does not put away the dishes after eating. So, the younger one always has to clean up the table after meals, and he feels uncomfortable. One day, after the elder one had eaten and was leaving, the younger one says, "You have to wash your own dishes." "You can wash them," the elder brother replied without hesitation and just went to his room. The younger one didn't like the situation, but his brother had already left.

The younger one knows that his elder brother is not in the habit of washing his own dishes. So, the younger can just serve the older with joy by washing all the dishes himself. Then, you might think the younger one will always have to wash the dishes, and the elder one won't try to mediate the problem. But if we act in goodness, God is the one who will make the changes. God will change the elder brother's heart so that he will think, 'I am sorry I made my brother wash dishes all the time. From now on, I will wash both my dishes and his.'

As in the illustration, if we follow the desires of the flesh just because of momentary benefit, we will always have discomfort and quarrels. But we will have joy if we serve others from the heart following the desires of the Holy Spirit.

The same principle applies in every other matter. Once you might have judged others with your own standards, but if you change your heart and understand others in goodness, you will have peace. How about when you meet with someone who has a very different personality from yours or someone whose opinions are very different from yours? Do you try to avoid him, or do you warmly greet him with a smile? In the view of unbelievers, it might be more comfortable for them to just avoid and ignore those whom they dislike than to try to be nice to them.

But those who follow the desires of the Holy Spirit will smile at such people with a heart of service. When we put ourselves to death every day with an intention to give comfort to others (1 Corinthians 15:31), we will experience that true peace and joy come from above. Furthermore, we will be able to enjoy peace and joy all the time, if we do not even have the feeling that we do not like somebody or somebody's personality does not match ours.

Suppose you get a call from a church leader to come with him to pay a visit to a church member who missed the Sunday service, or suppose you are asked to preach the gospel to a certain person on a holiday you rarely get. At one corner of your mind you want to take a rest, and another part of your mind suggests you want to do the work of God. It is up to your freewill to choose either way, but sleeping a lot and making your body comfortable does not necessarily give you joy.

You can feel the fullness of the Holy Spirit and joy when you give your time and possessions to doing the ministry of God. As you follow the desires of the Holy Spirit again and again, you will not only have increasingly more spiritual joy but also your heart will increasingly change into a heart of truth. To that same extent, you will bear the ripened fruit of joy, and your face will glow with spiritual light.

Third, we have to sow the seeds of joy and thanksgiving diligently.

For a farmer to reap the fruit of a harvest, he needs to sow the seeds and take care of them. In the same way, in order to bear the fruit of joy, we have to diligently look to the conditions of thanksgiving and offer the sacrifices of thanks to God. If we are God's children who have faith, there are so many things to rejoice about!

First, we have the joy of salvation that cannot be exchanged with anything. Also, the good God is our Father, and He keeps His children who live in the truth and answers whatever they ask. So, how happy are we? If we just keep the Lord's Day holy and give proper tithes, we will not face any disaster or accident throughout the whole year. If we do not commit sins and keep the commands of God, and work faithfully for His kingdom, then, we will always receive blessings.

Even if we might encounter some hardships, the solutions to all kinds of problems are found in the sixty-six books of the Bible. If the difficulty was caused by our own wrongdoings, we can repent and turn from such ways so that God will have mercy on us and give us the answer to solve the problem. When we look back on ourselves, if our heart does not condemn us, we can just rejoice and give thanks. Then, God will work out everything to make everything good and give us more blessings.

We should not take for granted the grace of God that He has given to us. We have to rejoice and give thanks to Him all the time. When we look for the conditions of thanksgiving and rejoice, God gives us more conditions of thanksgiving. In turn, our thanks and joy will increase, and eventually we will bear the fruit of joy completely.

Against Such Things There Is No Law

Mourning even after bearing the fruit of joy

Even though we bear the fruit of joy in our heart, we sometimes become sorrowful. It is spiritual mourning that is done in the truth.

First, there is mourning of repentance. If there are tests and trials caused by our sins, we cannot just rejoice and give thanks to solve the problem. If one can rejoice even after committing a sin, that joy is worldly joy that has nothing to do with God. In such a case, we have to repent with tears and turn from those ways. We have to thoroughly repent thinking, 'How could I commit such a sin believing in God? How could I forsake the grace of the Lord?' Then, God will accept our repentance, and as a proof that the barrier of sin is torn down, He will give us joy. We will feel so light and delighted as if flying into the sky, and a new kind of joy and thanksgiving come from above.

But mourning of repentance is certainly different from the tears of sorrow that are shed due to the pain caused by hardships or disasters. Even if you pray shedding so many tears and even with a runny nose, it is only fleshly mourning as long as you are weeping with resentment about your situations. Also, if you just try to escape from the problem fearing the punishment and do not turn from your sins completely, you cannot gain true joy. You will not feel that you are forgiven, either. If your mourning is true mourning of repentance, you have to cast away the willingness to commit sins itself and then bear the proper fruit of repentance. Only then will you receive the spiritual joy from above again.

Next, there is mourning that you have when God is disgraced

or for those souls who are going the way of death. It is a kind of mourning that is proper in the truth. If you have such mourning, you will pray for the kingdom of God very earnestly. You will ask for holiness and power to save more souls and expand the kingdom of God. Therefore, such mourning is pleasing and acceptable in the sight of God. If you have such spiritual mourning, the joy deep in your heart will not go away. You will not lose strength being gloomy or disheartened, but you will still have thanksgiving and happiness.

Several years ago, God showed to me the heavenly house of a person who prays for the kingdom of God and the church with a great deal of mourning. Her house was decorated with gold and precious gemstones, and especially there were many big, shiny pearls. As a pearl oyster makes a pearl with all its energy and sap, she mourned in prayer to resemble the Lord, and she mourned praying for the kingdom of God and the souls. God is paying her back for all her tearful prayers. Therefore, we should rejoice always believing in God, and we should also be able to mourn for the kingdom of God and the souls.

Be positive and follow goodness in all matters

When God created the first man, Adam, He gave joy in Adam's heart. But the joy Adam had at that time is different from the joy that we gain after going through human cultivation on this earth.

Adam was a living being, or a living spirit, which means he did not have any fleshly attributes, and thus he did not have any element that was opposite to joy. Namely, he did not have any concept of relativity to be able to realize the value of joy. Only those who have suffered diseases can understand how precious health is. Only those who have suffered poverty understand the true value of a rich life.

Adam had never experienced any pain, and he was not able to realize what a happy life he was living. Although he was enjoying an eternal life and the abundance of the Garden of Eden, he could not really rejoice from his heart. But after he ate from the tree of the knowledge of good and evil, flesh came into his heart, and he lost the joy that had been given by God. As he was going through many pains of this world, his heart was filled with sorrow, loneliness, resentment, hard feelings, and worries.

We have experienced all kinds of pains on this earth, and now we have to recover the spiritual joy that Adam had lost. In order to do this, we have to cast off flesh, follow the desires of the Holy Spirit all the time, and sow the seeds of joy and thanksgiving in all things. Here, if we add positive attitudes and follow goodness, we will be able to bear the fruit of joy completely.

This joy is gained after we have experienced the relative relationships of many things of this earth, unlike Adam who lived in the Garden of Eden. Therefore, the joy stems from the depth of our heart and it never changes. The true happiness we will enjoy in Heaven has already been cultivated in us on this earth. How are we going to be able to express the joy we will have when we finish our earthly life and go into the kingdom of heaven?

Luke 17:21 says, *"...nor will they say, 'Look, here it is!' or, 'There it is!' For behold, the kingdom of God is in your midst."* I hope you will quickly bear the fruit of joy in your heart so that you can taste Heaven on earth and lead a life always filled with happiness.

Joy

Hebrews 12:14

"Pursue peace with all men,

and the sanctification without

which no one will see the Lord."

Chapter 4

Peace

The fruit of peace
In order to bear the fruit of peace
Words of goodness are important
Think wisely from others' viewpoint
True peace in heart
Blessings for the peacemakers

Peace

The particles of salt are not visible, but when they crystallize, they become beautiful cubic crystals. A small amount of salt dissolves in water and changes the whole structure of the water. It is a seasoning which is absolutely necessary in cooking. The micro-elements in salt, in just a very small amount are crucially essential to sustain life functions.

Just as salt dissolves to add flavor to food and prevents rotting, God wants us to sacrifice ourselves to edify and purify others and bear the beautiful fruit of peace. Let us now look into the fruit of peace among the fruits of the Holy Spirit.

The fruit of peace

Even if they are believers in God, people cannot maintain peace with others as long as they have their ego, or 'self'. If they think their ideas are right, they tend to ignore others' opinions and act unbecomingly. Even though an agreement has been reached by the votes of the majority of the group, they keep on complaining about the decision. They would also look at the shortcomings of people rather than their good points. They could also speak ill of others and spread such things, thereby alienating people from each other.

When we are around such people we may feel like we are sitting on a bed of thorns and have no peace. Where there are peace-breakers, there are always problems, afflictions, and trials. If peace is broken in a country, family, a workplace, a church, or any group, the passageway for blessings will be blocked and there will be many difficulties.

In a play, the hero or heroine is of course important, but the other roles and the supporting work of each of the staff are also important. The same goes for all organizations. Even though it might seem to be something trivial, when each person does his job properly the task can be fully accomplished, and such a person can be entrusted with bigger roles later. Also, one must not be arrogant just because the job he is doing is important. When he also helps others grow up together, all the works can be accomplished peacefully.

Romans 12:18 says, *"If possible, so far as it depends on you, be at peace with all men."* And Hebrews 12:14 says, *"Pursue peace with all men, and the sanctification without which no one will see the Lord."*

Here, 'peace' is to be able to go along with the opinions of others, even if our opinions are correct. It is to give comfort to other people. It is a generous heart with which we can be OK with anything as long as it is within the boundary of the truth. It is to follow the benefit of others and not have any favoritism. It is trying to have no trouble or conflict with others by refraining from expressing opposing personal opinion and by not looking at the shortcomings of other people.

God's children must not only maintain peace between husbands and wives, parents and children, and brothers and neighbors, but they must also have peace with all people. They must have peace with not just those whom they love but with those who hate them and give them a hard time. It is especially important to maintain peace in the church. God cannot work if the peace is broken. It is only giving a chance to Satan to accuse us.

Also, even if we work hard and achieve great goals in the ministry of God, we cannot be praised if peace is broken.

In Genesis 26, Isaac maintained peace with everybody even in a situation where other people were challenging him. It was when Isaac, in an attempt to avoid famine, went to the place where the Philistines were living. He received blessings of God, and the number of his flocks and herds increased and he had a great household. The Philistines were jealous of him and stopped up Isaac's wells by filling them up with earth.

They did not have enough rain in that area, and especially in summer there was no rain. Wells were their lifelines. Isaac, however, did not quarrel or fight with them. He just left the place and dug another well. Whenever he found a well after a great deal of hardship, the Philistines came and insisted the well be theirs. Nevertheless, Isaac never protested and he just gave over the wells. He moved to another place and dug another well.

This cycle was repeated many times, but Isaac only treated those people with goodness, and God blessed him to get a well everywhere he went. Seeing this, the Philistines realized God was with him and did not bother him anymore. If Isaac had quarreled or fought with them because he was unfairly treated, he would have become their enemy and he would have had to leave that place. Even though he could have spoken up for himself in a fair and just manner, it wouldn't have worked since the Philistines were looking for a quarrel with evil intentions. For this reason, Isaac treated them with goodness and bore fruit of peace.

If we bear the fruit of peace in this way, God controls all the situations so that we can prosper in all things. Now, how can we bear this fruit of peace?

In order to bear the fruit of peace

First, we have to be at peace with God.

The most important thing in maintaining peace with God is that we must not have any walls of sin. Adam had to hide himself from God since he violated God's Word and ate the forbidden fruit (Genesis 3:8). In the past, he felt a very close intimacy with God, but now God's presence brought the feelings of fear and distance. It was because the peace with God had been broken due to his sin.

It is the same with us. When we act in the truth, we can be at peace with God and have confidence before God. Of course, in order to have complete and perfect peace, we have to cast off all sins and evil from our heart and become sanctified. But even though we are not perfect yet, as long as we practice the truth diligently within the measure of our faith, we can have peace with God. We cannot have perfect peace with God right from the beginning, but we can have peace with God when we try to follow peace with Him within the measure of our faith.

Even when we try to have peace with people, we must pursue peace with God first. Though we have to pursue peace with our parents, children, spouses, friends, and co-workers, we must never do anything that is against the truth. Namely, we must not break peace with God to follow peace with men.

For example, what if we bow down before idols or violate the

Lord's Day in order to have peace with unbelieving family members? It seems we have peace for the moment, but in fact we have seriously broken peace with God by creating a wall of sin before God. We cannot commit sins to have peace with people. Also, if we violate the Lord's Day to attend the wedding of a family member or a friend, it is to break peace with God, and after all, we cannot have true peace with those people either.

For us to have true peace with men, we first have to please God. Then, God will drive away the enemy devil and Satan and change the minds of the evil persons so that we can have peace with everybody. Proverbs 16:7 says, *"When a man's ways are pleasing to the LORD, He makes even his enemies to be at peace with him."*

Of course, the other person might keep on breaking peace with us even though we try our best within the truth. In such a case, if we react within the truth until the end, God will eventually work for the best of everything. It was the case with David and King Saul. Due to his jealousy King Saul tried to kill David, but David treated him with goodness until the end. David had multiple numbers of chances to kill him, but he chose to pursue peace with God following goodness. Finally, God let David sit on the throne to pay back his good deeds.

Second, we must have peace with ourselves.

In order to have peace with ourselves, we must cast away all forms of evil and become sanctified. As long as we have evil in our heart, our evilness will be agitated according to different situations, and thus peace will be broken. We might think we have peace when things are going well as we thought they would be,

Peace

but the peace is broken when things are not good and they affect our evilness in heart. When hatred or anger is boiling in our heart, how uncomfortable it is! But we can have peace of heart, no matter what the circumstances, if we keep on choosing the truth.

Some people, however, do not have true peace in their hearts though they try to practice the truth to have peace with God. It is because they have self-righteousness and the frameworks of their personality.

For example, some people do not have peace of mind because they are too bound by the Word of God. Just like Job before he went through the trials, they pray hard and try to live by the Word of God, but they are not doing these things with their love for God. They live by the Word of God out of fear of the punishments and retribution of God. And if by chance they should violate the truth in some circumstance, they become very nervous fearing that they might face unfavorable consequences.

In such a case, how afflicted their heart would be even though they are diligently practicing the truth! So, their spiritual growth stops or they lose the joy. After all, they are suffering because of their own self-righteousness and frameworks of thoughts. In this case, rather than being obsessed with the acts of keeping the law, they have to try to cultivate love for God. One can enjoy true peace if he loves God with all his heart and realizes God's love.

Here is another example. Some people do not have peace with themselves because of their negative thinking. They try to practice the truth, but they condemn themselves and cause pain in their own heart if they do not get the result they want to. They feel sorry before God and they lose heart thinking they lack so much.

They lose peace thinking, 'What if people around me are disappointed in me? What if they forsake me?"

Such people must become spiritual children. The thinking of those children who believe in the love of their parents is quite simple. Even if they make mistakes, they do not hide from their parents, but go into the bosom of their parents saying they will do better. If they say they are sorry and they will do better with a lovingly trusting face, it would probably cause the parents to smile even though they were attempting to scold their children.

Of course, it does not mean you should just say you will do better all the time and keep on making the same mistake. If you truly desire to turn from sins and do better next time, why would God turn His face away from you? Those who truly repent do not lose heart or become discouraged because of other people. Of course, they might have to receive punishments or be placed in a lowly place for some time according to justice. Nevertheless, if they are really certain of the love of God towards them, they can willingly accept the punishments of God and they do not care about other people's views or comments.

On the contrary, God is not pleased if they keep on doubting, thinking they were not forgiven of their sins. If they have truly repented and turned from their ways, it is pleasing in the sight of God to believe that they are forgiven. Even if there are trials caused by their wrongdoings, they will turn into blessings if they accept them with joy and thanksgiving.

Therefore, we must believe that God loves us even though we are not perfect yet, and He will make us perfect if we just keep on trying to change ourselves. Also, if we are lowered in a trial, we have to trust in God who will lift us up eventually. We must not feel impatient with a desire to be recognized by people. If we just keep on storing up truthful heart and deeds, we can have peace with ourselves as well as spiritual confidence.

Third, we should have peace with everyone.

In order to pursue peace with everybody, we must be able to sacrifice ourselves. We have to sacrifice for others, even to the point of giving our lives. Paul said, "I die daily," and just as he said, we must not insist on our things, our viewpoints, or preferences to have peace with everybody.

To have peace, we should not act unbecomingly or try to flaunt and boast of ourselves. We have to humble ourselves from the heart and lift others up. We shouldn't be biased, and at the same time, we should be able to accept different ways of others, that is, if it is within the truth. We should not think with the measure of our own faith but from the viewpoint of others. Even though our opinion is correct, or perhaps even better, we should still be able to follow others' opinions.

It does not mean, however, that we should just leave them be and go their way even though those other people are going the way of death by committing sins. Nor should we compromise with them or join with them in practicing the untruths. We should sometimes advise them or admonish them with love. We can receive great blessings when we pursue peace within the truth.

Next, to have peace with everybody we must not insist on our self-righteousness and frameworks. 'Frameworks' are what one thinks is right from within one's own individual personality, sense of propriety and preference. 'Self-righteousness' here is seeking to force on others one's personal opinions, beliefs and ideas that one considers to be superior. Self-righteousness and frameworks are shown in various forms in our lives.

What if a person violates the regulations of the company to justify his actions thinking to himself the regulations are wrong? He may think he is doing what is proper, but obviously his boss or co-workers would think otherwise. Also, it is in accordance with the truth to follow others' opinions as long as they are not untruths.

Each individual has a different personality because each one has been raised in different environments. Each one has received different education and measures of faith. So, each person has a different standard of judging right or wrong and good or bad. One person may think a certain thing is correct while another thinks it is wrong.

Let us talk about the relationship between a husband and a wife for example. The husband wants the house to be always maintained neatly, but the wife doesn't do it. The husband bears with it with love in the beginning and does the cleaning himself. But as this goes on, he gets frustrated. He begins to think his wife didn't get a proper home education. He wonders why she cannot do something that is so simple and proper. He does not understand why her habits do not change even after many years, despite his frequent advice.

But on the other hand, the wife has something to say as well. Her disappointment mounts toward her husband thinking, 'I don't exist just to clean and do housework. Sometimes if I cannot do the cleaning, he ought to do it himself. Why does he complain about it so much? It seemed like he was willing to do anything for me before, but now he complains over such trivial matters. He's even talking about my family education!' If each of them insists on their own opinions and desires, they cannot have peace. Peace can be established only when they consider the other's point of view and serve each other, and not when they think only with their own viewpoints.

Jesus told us that, when we give our offerings to God, if we have something against one of our brothers, we first have to be reconciled to him and then go back to make the offering. (Matthew 5:23-24). Our offerings will be accepted by God only after we have peace with that brother and give the offering.

Those who have peace with God and with themselves will not break peace with others. They wouldn't quarrel with anybody because they must have already cast away their greed, arrogance, pride, and self-righteousness and frameworks. Even when others are evil and they cause troubles, these people would sacrifice themselves to finally make peace.

Words of goodness are important

There are a couple of things that we must consider when we try to pursue peace. It is very important to speak only good words to maintain peace. Proverbs 16:24 says, *"Pleasant words are a honeycomb, sweet to the soul and healing to the bones."* Good words give strength and courage to those who are disheartened.

Against Such Things There Is No Law

They can become good medicine to revive dying souls.

On the contrary, evil words break peace. When Rehoboam, son of King Solomon, ascended to the throne, the people of the ten tribes asked the king to reduce their hard labor. The king answered, *"My father made your yoke heavy, but I will add to it; my father disciplined you with whips, but I will discipline you with scorpions"* (2 Chronicles 10:14). Because of these words, the king and the people were estranged from each other, which eventually resulted in the country splitting in two.

Man's tongue is a very small part of the body, but it has tremendous power. It is much like a small flame that can become a big fire and cause a great deal of damage if not controlled. For this reason James 3:6 says, *"And the tongue is a fire, the very world of iniquity; the tongue is set among our members as that which defiles the entire body, and sets on fire the course of our life, and is set on fire by hell."* Also, Proverbs 18:21 says, *"Death and life are in the power of the tongue, and those who love it will eat its fruit."*

Especially, if we speak words of resentment or complaints due to differences in opinions, they contain ill-feelings, and thus, the enemy devil and Satan bring accusations because of them. Also, just harboring complaints and resentments and revealing such feelings outwardly as words and actions are very different. Holding an ink bottle in your pocket is one thing, but opening the lid and pouring it out is quite another. If you pour it out, it will stain people around you as well as yourself.

In the same way, when you do the work of God, you might complain just because some things are not in agreement with your ideas. Then, some others who agree with your ideas will speak in the same way. If the number increases to two and three, it becomes a synagogue of Satan. The peace will be broken in the church and the church growth stops. Therefore, we always have to see, hear, and speak only good things (Ephesians 4:29). We must not even hear the words that are not of the truth or goodness.

Think wisely from others' viewpoint

What we have to consider secondly is a case where you do not have any hard feelings against the other person, but that person is breaking peace. Here, you have to think about whether it is really the other person's fault. Sometimes, you are the cause of the reasons for others to break peace without you realizing it.

You might hurt others' feelings due to your inconsideration or unwise words or behaviors. In such a case, if you keep on thinking you do not harbor any hard feelings against the other person, you can neither have peace with that person nor come to a self-realization that enables you to change. You should be able to check whether you are really a peacemaker even in the sight of the other person.

From a leader's point of view, he might think he is maintaining peace but his workers might be having a hard time. They cannot openly express their feelings to their superiors. They can only bear with it and hurt inside.

There is a famous episode about the Prime Minister Hwang Hee of Chosun Dynasty. He saw a farmer who was plowing his field with two bulls. The minister asked the farmer with a loud voice, "Which one of the two bulls works harder?" The farmer suddenly held the arms of the minister and took him to a distant place. He whispered in his ears, "The black one is sometimes lazy, but the yellow one works hard." "Why did you have to bring me here and whisper into my ears to talk about the bulls?" Hwang Hee asked with a smile on his face. The farmer replied, "Even the animals do not like it when we talk something bad about them." It is said Hwang Hee then realized his inconsiderations.

What if the two bulls understood what the farmer said? The yellow bull would have become arrogant, and the black bull would have been jealous to cause problems for the yellow bull or it would have gotten discouraged and worked less than before.

From this story, we can learn consideration even for animals, and we should be careful not to speak any words or show any actions that could be favoritism. Where there is favoritism, there is jealousy and arrogance. For example, if you praise just one person before many people, or if you reprimand only one person in front of many people, then you are laying the grounds for the rise of dissension. You should be careful and wise enough not to cause such problems.

Also, there are people who suffer because of the favoritism and discrimination of their bosses, and yet when they themselves become the boss, they discriminate against certain individuals and show favoritism towards others. But we understand that if you suffered from such injustice, you should be careful in your words and behaviors so that peace will not be broken.

True peace in heart

Another thing you should think about when accomplishing peace is that true peace must be accomplished within the heart. Even those who do not have peace with God or with themselves can have peace with other people to some extent. Many believers always hear that they must not break peace, so they might be able to control their hard feelings and not collide with others who have opinions that are different from their own. But not having an outward conflict does not mean they have borne the fruit of peace. The fruit of the Spirit is borne not only on the outside but in the heart.

For example, if the other person does not serve you or recognize you, you feel resentful, but you may not express it outwardly. You may think, 'I have to have just a little more patience!' and try to serve that person. But suppose the same thing happens again.

Then, you may accumulate resentment. You cannot directly express the resentment thinking it will only hurt your pride, but you might indirectly criticize that person. In some way you may reveal your sense of being persecuted. Sometimes, you do not understand others and that prevents having peace with them. You just keep your mouth shut fearing that you may have quarrels if you argue. You just stop talking to that person looking down on him thinking, 'He is evil and so self-insistent that I cannot talk with him.'

This way, you do not break peace outwardly, but you do not have good feelings towards that person either. You do not agree with his opinions, and you may even feel you do not want to be

Against Such Things There Is No Law

around him. You might even complain about him by talking to others about his shortcomings. You mention your uncomfortable feelings saying, "He is really evil. How can anyone understand him and what he did! But acting in goodness, I still put up with him." Of course, it is better not to break peace in this way than to directly break peace.

But in order to have true peace, you have to serve others from the heart. You should not suppress such feelings and still want to be served. You should have the willingness to serve and to seek the benefit of others.

You should not just smile on the outside while passing judgment on the inside. You have to understand others from their point of view. Only then can the Holy Spirit work. Even while they are seeking their own, they will be moved in their hearts and change. When each person involved has shortcomings, each one can assume the blame. Eventually, everybody can have true peace and be able to share their hearts.

Blessings for the peacemakers

Those who have peace with God, with themselves, and with everyone, have the authority to drive away darkness. So, they can accomplish peace around them. As written in Matthew 5:9, *"Blessed are the peacemakers, for they shall be called sons of God,"* they have the authority of the children of God, the authority of light.

For example, if you are a church leader, you can help the believers to bear the fruit of peace. Namely, you can provide them

63

with the Word of truth having authority and power, so they can depart from sins and break down their self-righteousness and frameworks. When synagogues of Satan are created that alienate people from one another, you can destroy them with the power of your word. This way, you can bring about peace among different people.

John 12:24 says, *"Truly, truly, I say to you, unless a grain of wheat falls into the earth and dies, it remains alone; but if it dies, it bears much fruit."* Jesus sacrificed Himself and died like a grain of wheat and bore countless fruits. He forgave the sins of countless dying souls and let them have peace with God. As a result, the Lord Himself became the King of kings and Lord of lords receiving great honor and glory.

We can gain abundant harvest only when we sacrifice ourselves. God the Father wants His beloved children to make sacrifice and 'die like wheat' to bear abundant fruit just like Jesus did. Jesus also said in John 15:8, *"My Father is glorified by this, that you bear much fruit, and so prove to be My disciples."* As said, let us follow the desires of the Holy Spirit to bear the fruit of peace and to lead many souls to the way of salvation.

Hebrews 12:14 says, *"Pursue peace with all men, and the sanctification without which no one will see the Lord."* Even if you are absolutely right, if others are having uncomfortable feelings because of you and if there are conflicts, it is not right in the sight of God, and thus, you should look back on yourself. Then, you can become a holy person who has no forms of evil and who is able to see the Lord. In doing so, I hope you will enjoy the spiritual authority on this earth by being called sons of God, and

64

get to an honorable position in Heaven where you can see the Lord all the time.

James 1:4

"And let endurance have its perfect result,

so that you may be perfect and complete,

lacking in nothing."

Chapter 5

Patience

Patience

So often it seems happiness in life depends on whether we can be patient or not. Between parents and children and husbands and wives, among siblings and with friends, people do the things they will regret very much because they are not patient. The success and failure in our studying, work, or business might also depend on our patience. Patience is such an important element in our lives.

Spiritual patience and what is thought to be patience by worldly people are decidedly different from each other. People in this world endure with patience, but it is fleshly patience. If they have hard feelings, they suffer so much trying to suppress them. They might clinch their teeth or even stop eating. Eventually it leads to problems of nervousness or depression. Yet they say such people who can suppress their feelings well show great patience. But this is not spiritual patience at all.

Patience that does not need to be patient

Spiritual patience is not to be patient with evil but only with goodness. If you are patient with goodness, you can overcome hardships with thanksgiving and hope. This will lead to having a broader heart. On the contrary, if you are patient with evil, your ill-feelings will pile up and your heart will increasingly become rougher.

Suppose somebody is cursing you and causing you pain without a cause. You might feel your pride is hurt and even feel victimized, but you can also suppress it thinking you should be patient according to the Word of God. But your face turns red, your breathing becomes faster, and your lips tighten as you try to control your thoughts and emotions. If you suppress feelings this way, they might spring up later if things get worse. Such patience is not spiritual patience.

If you have spiritual patience, your heart will not be agitated by anything. Even if you are wrongfully accused of something, you just try to let other people be at ease thinking there must be some kind of a misunderstanding. If you have such a heart, you would not need to 'endure' or 'forgive' anybody. Let me give you an easy illustration.

On a cold winter night, a certain house had the lights on until late hours. The baby in the house had a fever that was going up to 40 °C (104 °F). The child's father soaked his T-shirt with cold water and held the baby. When the father put a cold towel on the baby it surprised him and he did not like it. But the baby was comforted in the arms of his father, although the T-shirt felt cold for a moment.

When the T-shirt became warm due to the fever of the baby, the father would wet it again with cold water. The father had to wet his T-shirt scores of times before morning came. But he did not seem to have any tiredness. But rather he was looking with loving eyes at his baby who was asleep in the security of his arms.

Even though he had been up all night, he had no complaints of hunger or tiredness. He did not have the leisure of thinking of his own body. All his attention was focused on the baby and thinking of how to make his son feel better and more comfortable. And when the baby did get better, he did not think of his own toil. When we love somebody, we can automatically endure hardships and toil, and therefore, we would not need to be patient about anything. This is the spiritual meaning of 'patience'.

The fruit of patience

We can find 'patience' in 1 Corinthians chapter 13, the "Love Chapter", and this is the patience to cultivate love. For example, it says that love does not seek its own. In order to give up what we want and seek the benefit of others first according to this word, we will face the situations that require our patience. The patience in the "Love Chapter" is the patience to cultivate love.

But the patience that is one of the fruits of the Holy Spirit is patience in everything. This patience is a level higher than the patience in spiritual love. There are difficulties when we try to achieve a goal, whether it is for the kingdom of God or personal sanctification. There will be mourning and toil expending all our energy. But we can patiently endure with faith and love because we have the hope to reap the fruit. This kind of patience is the patience as one of the fruits of the Holy Spirit. There are three aspects to this patience.

The first is the patience to change our heart.
The more evil we have in heart, the more difficult it is to be patient. If we have measures of anger, arrogance, greed, self-righteousness and self-made frameworks, we will have tempers and hard feelings that can rise over trivial matters.

There was a church member whose monthly income was about 15,000 US dollars, and in a certain month his income was much less than usual. Then, he begrudgingly complained against God. Later he confessed that he was not grateful for the affluence he had been enjoying because he had greed in his heart.

We should be thankful for everything God has given to us,

71

even though we do not make so much money. Then, greed will not grow in our heart and we will be able to receive blessings of God.

But as we cast away evil and become sanctified, it becomes easier and easier to be patient. We can endure quietly even in difficult situations. We can just understand and forgive others without having to suppress anything.

Luke 8:15 says, *"But the seed in the good soil, these are the ones who have heard the word in an honest and good heart, and hold it fast, and bear fruit with perseverance."* Namely, those who have good hearts like good soil, can be patient until they bear good fruits.

However we still need endurance and we need to put in effort to change our hearts into the good soil. Holiness cannot be automatically achieved just by our desire to have it. We have to make ourselves obedient to the truth by praying fervently with all our hearts and with fasting. We have to quit what we once loved, and if something is not spiritually beneficial, we have to cast it away. We must not stop in the middle or just quit trying after trying it a couple of times. Until we reap the fruit of sanctification completely and until we achieve our goal, we have to do our best with self-control and acting by the Word of God.

The ultimate destination of our faith is the kingdom of heaven, and especially, the most beautiful dwelling place, New Jerusalem. We have to keep on going with diligence and patience until we reach our destination.

But sometimes, we see cases in which people experience a slow down in the speed of sanctifying their hearts after leading a diligent Christian life.

They cast away the 'works of the flesh' quickly because they are the sins that are observable on the outside. But because the 'things of the flesh' are not seen on the outside, how fast they cast them off is slowed down. When they find the untruth in them, they pray hard to cast it away, but they just forget about it after several days. If you want to remove a weed completely, you do not just pluck the leaf, but you have to pull out its root. The same principle applies to sinful natures. You have to pray and change your heart until the end, until you pull out the root of the sinful natures.

When I was a new believer, I prayed to cast away certain sins, because I understood while reading the Bible that God hates the sinful attributes such as hatred, temper, and arrogance very much. When I determinedly adhered to my self-centered perspectives, I could not cast away hatred and ill-feelings from my heart. But in prayer God gave me grace to understand others from their standpoints. All my hard feelings against them melted away and my hatred was gone.

I learned to be patient as I cast off anger. In a situation where I was wrongfully accused, I counted in my mind, 'one, two, three, four...' and held the words I wanted to speak out. At first, it was difficult to hold my temper, but as I kept on trying, my anger and irritation gradually went away. Eventually, even in a very anger-provoking situation, I did not have anything that was coming up from my mind.

I believe it took three years to cast off arrogance. When I was a novice in faith I did not even know what arrogance was, but I just prayed to cast it off. I kept on checking myself while praying. As a result, I was able to respect and honor even the people who seemed to be inferior to me in many aspects. Later, I came to serve other fellow pastors with the same attitude whether they were in leadership positions or just newly ordained. After patiently praying for three years, I realized I did not have any attributes of arrogance in me, and from that time on I did not have to pray about arrogance any longer.

If you do not pull out the root of the sinful nature, that particular attribute of sin will come up in an extreme situation. You might be disappointed when you realize that you still have the characters of untruthful heart which you thought you had already cast off. You might be discouraged thinking, 'I tried so hard to cast it off, but it is still there in me.'

You may find forms of untruth in you until you pull out the original root of sinful nature, but it doesn't mean you didn't make spiritual progress. When you peel an onion, you can see the same kind of layers come again and again. But if you keep on peeling without stopping, the onion will finally disappear. It's the same with sinful natures. You must not get discouraged just because you didn't completely cast them away yet. You have to have patience until the end and continue to try even harder while looking forward to seeing yourself having changed.

Some other people get discouraged if they don't receive material blessings immediately after they act by the Word of God. They think they don't receive anything in return except a loss when they act in goodness. Some people even complain that they attend church diligently but do not receive blessings. Of course, there are no reasons to complain. It is just that they do not receive the blessings of God because they are still practicing untruths and not casting away the things that God tells us to cast away.

The fact that they are complaining proves that the focus of their faith is misplaced. You don't get tired if you act in goodness and truth with faith. The more you act in goodness, the more joyous you become, so you come to long for more of the things of goodness. When you become sanctified by faith in this way, your soul will prosper, all things go well with you, and you will be healthy.

Second kind of patience is that among men.

When you have interaction with people who have different personalities and educations, you may have situations arise. Especially, a church is a place where people from a vast range of backgrounds gather. So, beginning with trivial matters to great and serious matters, you may have different thoughts, and peace might be broken as well.

Then, people might say, "His way of thinking is completely different from mine. It is difficult for me to work with him because we have very different personalities." But even between husband and wife, how many couples would have perfectly matching personalities? Their life habits and tastes are different, but they have to yield to each other to be befitting one another.

Those who long for sanctification will be patient in any kind of situation with any kind of person and maintain peace. Even in some difficult and uncomfortable situations, they try to be

Patience

accommodating to others. They always understand others with a good heart and they endure while seeking the benefit of others. Even when others act with evil, they just bear with them. They pay back this evil only with goodness, and not with evil.

We also have to be patient when we evangelize or counsel the souls, or when we train church workers to accomplish the kingdom of God. While doing a pastoral ministry, I see some people whose changes take place very slowly. When they befriend the world and disgrace God, I shed many tears in mourning, but I have never given up on them from my side. I always bear with them for I have the hope that they will someday change.

When I raise the church workers, I have to be patient for such a long time. I cannot just direct all subordinates or force them to do what I want. Even though I know that the things will be accomplished a little more slowly, I cannot take away the duty from the church workers, saying, "You are not capable enough. You are fired." I just bear with them and guide them until they become capable. I wait for them for five, ten, or fifteen years so that they can have the ability to fulfill their duties through spiritual training.

Not just when they don't bear any fruit, but also when they do things wrong, I endure with them so they won't stumble. It might be easier if another person who has the capability just does it for them, or if that person is replaced with somebody who is more capable. But the reason why I endure until the end is for each of the souls. It is also to accomplish the kingdom of God more completely.

If you sow the seed of patience in this way, you will certainly gain the fruit according to the justice of God. For example, if you

Against Such Things There Is No Law

endure with some souls until they change, praying for them with tears, you will have the broad heart to harbor all of them. So, you will gain the authority and power to revive many souls. You will gain the power to change the souls you harbor in your heart through the prayer of a righteous man. Also, if you control your heart and sow the seed of endurance even in the face of false accusations, God will let you reap the fruit of blessings.

Third is the patience in our relation with God.

It refers to the patience that you should have until you receive the answer to your prayer. Mark 11:24 says, *"Therefore I say to you, all things for which you pray and ask, believe that you have received them, and they will be granted you."* We can believe all the words in the sixty-six books of the Bible if we have faith. There are promises of God that we will receive what we ask for, and therefore we can achieve anything with prayer.

But of course, it does not mean we can just pray and do nothing. We have to practice the Word of God in a way for us to be able to receive the answer. For example, a student whose grades are ranked around middle in his class prays to become the top student. But he daydreams in his classes and he does not study. Will he be able to become the top in his class? He has to study hard while praying hard so that God can help him become the top of his class.

The same goes for doing businesses. You earnestly pray for your business to thrive, but your goal is to have another house, invest in real estate, and get a luxurious car. Would you be able to receive the answer to your prayer? Of course, God wants His children to live a life in abundance, but God cannot be pleased with prayers that ask for things to fulfill one's greed. But if you want to receive blessings to help the needy and support the missionary works, and if you follow the right way without doing anything illegal, God will certainly lead you to the way of blessings.

There are many promises in the Bible that God will answer His children's prayers. But in many cases people don't receive their answers because they are not patient enough. Men may ask for an immediate response, but God may not answer them immediately.

God answers them at the most appropriate and opportune time because He knows everything. If the subject of their prayer request is something big and important, God can answer them only when the amount of prayer is filled. When Daniel prayed to receive the revelation of spiritual things, God sent His angel to answer that prayer as soon as Daniel began to pray. But it took a period of twenty one days before Daniel actually met with the angel. For those twenty one days Daniel kept praying with the same earnest heart as when he had started praying. If we really believe that we have already been given something, then it's not difficult waiting to receive it. We will just think about the joy that we will have when we actually receive the solutions of the problem.

Some believers cannot wait until they receive what they ask God in prayer. They may pray and fast to ask God, but if the answer doesn't come quickly enough, they may just give up thinking God isn't going to answer them.

If we really believed and prayed, we wouldn't become disheartened or give up. We do not know when the answer will come: tomorrow, tonight, after the next prayer, or after a year.

God knows the perfect timing to give us the answer.

James 1:6-8 says, *"But he must ask in faith without any doubting, for the one who doubts is like the surf of the sea, driven and tossed by the wind. For that man ought not to expect that he will receive anything from the Lord, being a double-minded man, unstable in all his ways."*

The only important thing is how firmly we believe when we pray. If we really believe that we have already received an answer, we can be happy and glad in any kind of situation. If we have the faith to receive the answer, we will pray and act with faith until the fruit is given into our hands. Furthermore, when we go through afflictions of heart or persecutions while doing the work of God, we can bear fruits of goodness only through patience.

Patience of fathers of faith

There would be difficult moments when running a marathon race. And the joy of finishing the course after overcoming such difficult moments would be so great it can be understood only by those who have experienced it. God's children who run the race of faith might also face difficulties from time to time, but they can overcome anything by looking up to Jesus Christ. God will give them His grace and strength, and the Holy Spirit will also help them.

Hebrews 12:1-2 says, *"Therefore, since we have so great a cloud of witnesses surrounding us, let us also lay aside every encumbrance and the sin which so easily entangles us, and let us run with endurance the race that is set before us, fixing our eyes on Jesus, the author and perfecter of faith, who for the joy set before Him endured the cross, despising the shame, and has sat down at the right hand of the throne of God."*

Jesus suffered a great deal of contempt and mockeries from His creatures until He fulfilled the providence of salvation. But because He knew that He was going to sit on the right hand of God's throne and that salvation would be given to the mankind, He endured until the end without thinking about the physical shame. After all, He died on the cross taking the sins of the mankind, but He resurrected on the third day to open the way of salvation. God established Jesus as the King of kings and Lord of lords for He obeyed until death with love and faith.

Jacob was a grandson of Abraham and he became the father of the nation of Israel. He had a persistent heart. He took the birthright of his brother Esau by cheating him, and he fled to Haran. He received the promise of God in Bethel.

Genesis 28:13-15 says, *"...the land on which you lie, I will give it to you and to your descendants. Your descendants will also be like the dust of the earth, and you will spread out to the west and to the east and to the north and to the south; and in you and in your descendants shall all the families of the earth be blessed. Behold, I am with you and will keep you wherever you go, and will bring you back to this land; for I will not leave you until I have done what I have promised you."* Jacob endured for twenty years in his trials and eventually became the father of all Israelites.

Joseph was the eleventh son of Jacob, and he received all the love of his father alone among other brothers. One day he was sold as a slave into Egypt by the hands of his own brothers. He became a slave in a foreign country, but he was not disheartened. He did his best in his work and he was recognized by his master for his faithfulness. His situations got better taking care of all the matters of his master's household, but he was wrongfully accused and put in a political prison. It was one trial after another.

Of course, all the steps were the grace of God in a process to prepare him to become the prime minister of Egypt. But nobody knew it except God. Still, Joseph was not discouraged even in the jail, because he had faith and he believed the promise of God given to him in his childhood. He believed that God would fulfill his dream in which the sun and the moon and eleven stars in the sky bowed down to him, and he was not swayed in any situation. He trusted God completely, and he endured in all matters and followed the right way according to the Word of God. His faith was true faith.

What if you were in the same situation? Can you imagine what he felt for 13 years since the day he was sold as a slave? You probably will pray so much before God to get out of the situation. You will probably check yourself and repent of all the things that you can think of in order to receive the answer from God. You will also ask for grace of God with many tears and earnest words. And if you don't get the answer for a year, two years, and even ten years, but you only get into more difficult situations, how would you feel?

He was jailed during the most vigorous years of his life and as he saw the days go by meaninglessly he might have felt so miserable if he had not had the faith that he had. If he had

Patience

thought of his good life in his father's house, he would have felt even more miserable. But Joseph always trusted God who was watching him, and he firmly believed in the love of God who gives the best at the right time. He never lost hope even in depressing trials, and he acted with faithfulness and goodness being patient until finally his dream came true.

David was also recognized by God as a man after God's own heart. But even after he was anointed as the next king, he had to go through so many trials including being chased by King Saul. He had many near-death situations. But by enduring all those difficulties with faith he became a great king who was able to rule over all Israel.

James 1:3-4 says, *"...knowing that the testing of your faith produces endurance. And let endurance have its perfect result, so that you may be perfect and complete, lacking in nothing."* I urge you to cultivate this patience completely. That patience will increase your faith and broaden and deepen your heart to make it more mature. You will experience the blessings and answers of God that He promised if you completely accomplish patience (Hebrews 10:36).

Patience to go to the heavenly kingdom

We need patience to go to the heavenly kingdom. Some say that they will enjoy the world when they are young and begin to attend church after they become old. Some others lead a diligent life of faith in hope of the Lord's coming, but then they lose patience and they change their minds. Because the Lord doesn't come as quickly as they expect, they feel that it is too difficult to continue to be diligent in faith. They say they will take a rest in circumcising their heart and doing God's work, and when they can be sure of seeing the sign of the Lord's coming, then they will try harder.

But nobody knows when God will call our spirit, or when the Lord will come. Even if we can know that time in advance, we cannot have faith as much as we want. Men cannot just have the spiritual faith to receive salvation as they want. It is given only by the grace of God. The enemy devil and Satan will not just leave them to receive salvation so easily either. Moreover if you have the hope to go into New Jerusalem in Heaven, you can do everything in patience.

Psalm 126:5-6 says, *"Those who sow in tears shall reap with joyful shouting. He who goes to and fro weeping, carrying his bag of seed, shall indeed come again with a shout of joy, bringing his sheaves with him."* There must certainly be our efforts, tears, and mourning while we sow the seeds and grow them. Sometimes, necessary rain might not come, or there could be hurricanes or too much rain to damage the crops. But at the end of it, we will surely have the joy of abundant harvest according to the rules of justice.

God waits a thousand years like a day to gain true children and He bore with the pain of giving His one and only Son for us. The Lord endured the suffering of the cross, and the Holy Spirit also bears with inexpressible groanings during the time of human cultivation. I hope you will cultivate complete, spiritual patience, remembering this love of God so that you will have fruits of blessings both on this earth and in Heaven.

Luke 6:36

"Therefore be merciful

as your Father also is merciful."

Chapter 6

Kindness

Kindness

At times people say that they cannot understand a certain person even though they've tried to understand him, or that though they have tried to forgive a person, they are unable to forgive him. But if we have borne the fruit of kindness in our heart, there is nothing that we cannot understand and there isn't anybody we cannot forgive. We will be able to understand any kind of person with goodness and accept any kind of person with love. We would not say we like one person because of a certain reason and we don't like another person because of another reason. We would not dislike nor hate anybody. We would not be on bad terms with or harbor hard feelings against anybody not to mention having enemies.

Understanding and forgiving others with the fruit of kindness

Kindness is the quality or state of being kind. But the spiritual meaning of kindness is somewhat closer to mercy. And, the spiritual meaning of mercy is "to understand in the truth even those who cannot be understood at all by men." It is also the heart that is able to forgive in the truth even those who cannot be forgiven by men. God shows compassion towards mankind with the heart of mercy.

Psalm 130:3 says, *"If You, LORD, should mark iniquities, O LORD, who could stand?"* As written, if God had no mercy and judged us according to justice, nobody would be able to stand before God. But God forgave and accepted even those who could be neither forgiven nor accepted if justice is applied strictly.

Furthermore, God gave the life of His one and only Son to save such men from eternal death. Since we have become God's children by believing in the Lord, God wants us to cultivate this heart of mercy. For this reason, God says in Luke 6:36, *"Be merciful, just as your Father is merciful."*

This mercy is somewhat similar to love but it is also different in various ways. Spiritual love is to be able to sacrifice oneself for others without any price put upon it, while mercy is more of forgiveness and acceptance. Namely, it is to be able to accept and embrace everything of a person and not misunderstand or hate him even though he is not worthy of receiving any love. You would not hate or avoid somebody just because his opinions are different from your own, but instead you can become strength and comfort to him. If you have the warm heart to accept others, you would not reveal their iniquities or wrongdoings but cover and accept them so that you can have a beautiful relationship with them.

There was an event which revealed this heart of mercy very vividly. One day Jesus prayed all night at Mount of Olives and came to the Temple in the morning. Many people gathered as He sat down, and there arose a commotion as He was preaching the Word of God. There were some scribes and Pharisees among the crowd who brought a woman before Jesus. She was shivering with fear.

They told Jesus that the woman was caught in the action of adultery, and asked Him what He would do to her since the Law says such a woman must be stoned to death. If Jesus told them to stone her, it was not in accordance with His teachings saying,

Against Such Things There Is No Law

"Love your enemies." But if He told them to forgive her, it was to violate the Law. It seemed Jesus was put in a very difficult situation. Jesus, however, just wrote something on the ground and said as recorded in John 8:7, *"He who is without sin among you, let him be the first to throw a stone at her."* People had pangs of conscience and left one by one. Eventually there remained only Jesus and the woman.

In John 8:11 Jesus said to her, *"I do not condemn you, either. Go. From now on sin no more."* Saying, "I do not condemn you," means He forgave her. Jesus forgave a woman who could not be forgiven and gave her a chance to turn from her sins. This is the heart of mercy.

Needing to have the heart and deeds like those of the Lord

Mercy is to truly forgive and to love even the enemies. Just like a mother cares for her newborn baby, we would accept and embrace everybody. Even when people have some great faults or they have committed grave sins, we will first have mercy rather than passing judgment and condemnation on them. We would hate the sins, but not the sinner; we will understand that person and try to let him live.

Suppose there is a child with a very frail body who gets sick often. How would the mother feel towards this child? She wouldn't wonder why he was born like that and why he gave her so much difficulty. She would not hate the child because of it. She would rather have more love and compassion towards him than other children who are healthy.

There was a mother whose son was mentally retarded. Until he reached the age of twenty his mental age was that of a two-year-old, and the mother could not take her eyes off of him. Nevertheless, she never thought it was difficult to take care of her son. She just felt sympathy and compassion for her son while caring for him. If we bear this kind of fruit of mercy completely, we will have mercy not just for our own children but for everybody.

Jesus preached the gospel of the kingdom of heaven during His public ministry. His main audiences were not the rich and powerful; but those who were poor, neglected, or those whom people considered sinners, such as tax-collectors or harlots.

It was the same when Jesus chose His disciples. People may think it would have been wise to choose the disciples from those who were thoroughly familiar with the Law of God, because it would be easier to teach them the Word of God. But Jesus did not choose such people. As His disciples He chose Matthew, who was a tax-collector; and Peter, Andrew, James, and John who were fishermen.

Jesus also healed various kinds of diseases. One day, He healed a person who had been ill for thirty-eight years and waiting for the moving of the waters at the pool of Bethesda. He was living in pain without having any hope of life, but nobody paid attention to him. But Jesus came to him and asked him, "Do you wish to get well?" and healed him.

Jesus also healed a woman who had been bleeding for twelve

90

years. He opened the eyes of Bartimaeus, who was a blind beggar (Matthew 9:20-22; Mark 10:46-52). On His way to a city called Nain, He saw a widow whose only son had died. He had pity on her and revived the dead son (Luke 7:11-15). In addition to these, He looked after those who were oppressed. He became friends to the neglected such as tax-collectors and sinners.

Some people criticized Him for He was eating with the sinners, saying, *"Why is your teacher eating with the tax collectors and sinners?"* (Matthew 9:11) But when Jesus heard this He said, *"It is not those who are healthy who need a physician, but those who are sick. But go and learn what this means: 'I desire compassion, and not sacrifice,' for I did not come to call the righteous, but sinners"* (Matthew 9:12-13). He taught us of the heart of compassion and mercy for the sinners and the sick.

Jesus did not only come for the rich and the righteous but mainly for the poor and the sick, and sinners. We can quickly bear the fruit of mercy when we take after this heart and the deeds of Jesus. Now, let us delve into what we should do specifically to bear the fruit of mercy.

Casting off prejudice to have kindness

Worldly people so often judge people by appearances. Their attitudes toward people change depending on whether or not they see them as rich or famous. God's children must not judge people by their appearances or change their attitudes of heart just because of appearances. We have to consider even little children or those who seem to be inferior to be better than ourselves and serve them with the heart of the Lord.

James 2:1-4 says, *"My brethren, do not hold your faith in our glorious Lord Jesus Christ with an attitude of personal favoritism. For if a man comes into your assembly with a gold ring and dressed in fine clothes, and there also comes in a poor man in dirty clothes, and you pay special attention to the one who is wearing the fine clothes, and say, 'You sit here in a good place,' and you say to the poor man, 'You stand over there, or sit down by my footstool,' have you not made distinctions among yourselves, and become judges with evil motives?"*

Also, 1 Peter 1:17 says, *"If you address as Father the One who impartially judges according to each one's work, conduct yourselves in fear during the time of your stay on earth."*

If we bear the fruit of mercy, we will not judge or condemn others by their appearances. We should also check whether we have prejudice or favoritism in a spiritual sense. There are some people who are slow to understand spiritual matters. Some others have some deficiencies of body, so they may speak or do some things that are out of context in certain situations. Still others act in a way that is not in accordance with the manners of the Lord.

When you see or interact with those people, haven't you felt somewhat frustrated? Have you not looked down on them or wanted to avoid them to some extent? Have you caused others embarrassment with your aggressive words or impolite attitudes?

Also, some people talk about and condemn another person as if they were in the seat of the judge when that person has committed a sin. When a woman who had committed adultery was brought to Jesus, many people pointed their fingers at her in judgment and condemnation. But Jesus did not condemn her but gave her a chance for salvation. If you have such a heart of mercy, then you will have compassion for those who are receiving punishments for their sins, and you will hope that they will overcome.

Mercy for those in difficulties

If we are merciful, we will have compassion on those who are in difficulties and enjoy helping them. We will not just feel pity in our hearts for them and say, "Take heart and be strong!" with only our lips. We will actually give some kind of help to them.

1 John 3:17-18 says, *"But whoever has the world's goods, and sees his brother in need and closes his heart against him, how does the love of God abide in him? Little children, let us not love with word or with tongue, but in deed and truth."* Also, James 2:15-16 says, *"If a brother or sister is without clothing and in need of daily food, and one of you says to them, 'Go in peace, be warmed and be filled,' and yet you do not give them what is necessary for their body, what use is that?"*

You should not think, 'It's a pity that he is starving, but I cannot really do anything because I have just enough for myself.' If you really feel pity with a true heart, you can share or even give your portion. If one thinks his situation does not allow for him to help any other people, then it is very unlikely he will help others even if he becomes rich.

This does not concern just material things. When you see

somebody who is suffering from any kind of problem, you should want to be of some help and share the pain with that person. This is mercy. Especially, you should care for those who are falling into Hell because they do not believe in the Lord. You will try your best to lead them to the way of salvation.

In Manmin Central Church, since its opening, there have been great works of God's power. But I still ask for greater power and dedicate all my life to manifesting that power. It's because I suffered from poverty myself, and I thoroughly experienced the pain of losing hope because of disease. When I see those people who suffer from these problems, I feel their pain as my own pain, and I want to help them the very best I can.

It is my desire to solve their problems and rescue them from the punishments of Hell and lead them to Heaven. But how can I alone help so many people? The answer I received to this is the power of God. Even though I cannot solve all the problems of poverty, diseases, and so many other things of all people, I can help them meet and experience God. That is why I am trying to manifest greater power of God, so more people can meet and experience God.

Of course, showing the power is not the completion of the process of salvation. Even though they come to have faith by seeing the power, we have to care for them physically and spiritually until they stand firmly on faith. That is why I did my best to provide aid to the needy even when our church itself had financial difficulties. It was so that they could march towards Heaven with more strength. Proverbs 19:17 says, *"One who is gracious to a poor man lends to the LORD, and He will repay*

Against Such Things There Is No Law

him for his good deed." If you take care of the souls with the heart of the Lord, God will certainly pay you back with His blessings.

Do not easily point out others' shortcomings

If we love somebody, we sometimes have to give advice or rebuke him. If the parents do not scold their children at all but forgive all the time just because they love their children, then the children will be spoiled. But if we have mercy we cannot easily punish, rebuke, or point out shortcomings. When we just give a word of advice, we will do it with prayerful mind and caring for that person's heart. Proverbs 12:18 says, *"There is one who speaks rashly like the thrusts of a sword, but the tongue of the wise brings healing."* Pastors and leaders in particular who are teaching the believers must keep these words in mind.

You may easily say, "You have an untruthful heart in you, and it doesn't please God. You have this and this shortcoming, and you are not loved by others because of these things." Even if what you say is true, if you point out shortcomings within your self-righteousness or frameworks without love, it doesn't give life. Others will not change as a result of the advice, in fact, their feelings will be hurt and they will become discouraged and lose strength.

Sometimes, some church members ask me to point out their shortcomings so they can realize them and change themselves. They say they want to realize their shortcomings and change. So, if I very carefully begin to say something, they stop my words to explain their standpoints, so I cannot really give the advice. Giving a piece of advice is not an easy thing anyway. For that moment, they can accept it with thanks, but if they lose the fullness of the Spirit, nobody knows what will happen in their heart.

Sometimes, I have to point out things in order to accomplish the kingdom of God or to allow for the people to receive the solution to their problems. I watch the mood on their faces with prayerful mind, hoping they will not be offended or discouraged.

Of course, when Jesus rebuked the Pharisees and the scribes with strong words, they were not able to accept His advice. Jesus was giving them a chance so that even just one among them might listen to Him and repent. Also, because they were the teachers of the people, Jesus wanted the people to come to a realization and not be deceived by their hypocrisy. Other than such special cases, you should not speak words that might offend others' feelings or uncover their iniquities so they will stumble. When you have to give advice because it is absolutely necessary, you should do it with love, thinking from the other's viewpoint and with care for that soul.

Be generous to everybody

Most people can generously give what they have to some extent to those whom they love. Even those who are stingy can lend or give presents to others if they know they can receive something back in return. In Luke 6:32 it says, *"If you love those who love you, what credit is that to you? For even sinners love those who love them."* We can bear the fruit of mercy when we can give of ourselves without wanting anything in return.

Jesus knew from the beginning that Judas would betray Him, but He treated him in the same way He treated the other disciples. He gave him many chances again and again so he could come to repentance. Even when He was being crucified, Jesus prayed for those who were crucifying Him. Luke 23:34 says, *"Father, forgive them; for they do not know what they are doing."* This is the mercy with which we can forgive even those who cannot be forgiven at all.

In the book of Acts, we can find Stephen also had this fruit of mercy. He was not an apostle, but he was filled with grace and power of God. Great signs and wonders took place through him. Those who did not like this fact tried to argue with him, but when he answered with the wisdom of God in the Holy Spirit, they could not counter-argue. It says people saw his face, and it was like that of an angel (Acts 6:15).

The Jews had pangs of conscience listening to the sermon of Stephen, and they eventually took him outside the city and stoned him to death. Even while he was dying, he prayed for those who were throwing stones at him saying, *"Lord, do not hold this sin against them!"* (Acts 7:60) This shows us that he had already forgiven them. He had no hatred against them, but he only had the fruit of mercy having compassion on them. Stephen could manifest such great works because he had such a heart.

Then how well have you cultivated this kind of heart? Is there still somebody you don't like or somebody who is not on good terms with you? You should be able to accept and embrace others even though their characters and opinions are not in agreement with yours. You should first think from that person's viewpoint. Then, you can change the feelings of dislike toward that person.

If you just think, 'Why on earth does he do that? I just can't understand him,' then, you will only have hard feelings and you will have uncomfortable feelings when you see him. But if you can think, 'Ah, in his position he can act this way,' then, you can change the feelings of dislike. Now, you will rather have mercy on that person who can't help but do that, and you will pray for him.

As you change your thoughts and feelings this way, you can pull out the hatred and other evil feelings one by one. If you keep the feeling that you want to insist on your stubbornness, you cannot accept others. Neither can you pull out the hatred or hard feelings in you. You should cast away your self-righteousness and change your thoughts and feelings so that you can accept and serve any kind of person.

Attribute the honor to others

In order to bear the fruit of mercy, we should give the honor to others when something is done well, and we should accept the blame when something goes wrong. When the other person receives all the recognition and is praised more even though you worked together, you still can rejoice with him like it was your own happiness. You will not have any discomfort thinking you did more work and that person is praised even though he has many shortcomings. You will only be thankful thinking that he can have more confidence and work harder after being praised by others.

If the mother does something with her child, and only the

child receives the reward, what would the mother feel? There shouldn't be any mothers who complain saying that she helped her child do the work properly and she didn't get any reward. Also, it is good for a mother to hear from others that she is beautiful, but she would be happier if people say her daughter is beautiful.

If we have the fruit of mercy, we can put any other person ahead of us and attribute the merit to him. And we will rejoice together with him as if we ourselves were praised. Mercy is the characteristic of God the Father who is full of compassion and love. Not only mercy, but each of the fruits of the Holy Spirit is also the heart of the perfect God. Love, joy, peace, patience, and all other fruits are the different aspects of God's heart.

Therefore, to bear the fruits of the Holy Spirit means we have to strive to have the heart of God in us and be perfect as God is perfect. The more ripened the spiritual fruits become in you, the lovelier you will become, and God will not be able to contain His love for you. He will rejoice over you saying you are His sons and daughters who resemble Him so much. If you become God's children who please Him, you can receive anything you ask in prayer, and even the things that you just harbor in your heart, God knows them and answers you. I hope all of you will bear the fruits of the Holy Spirit completely and please God in all things, so that you will be overflowing with blessings and enjoy great honor in the kingdom of heaven as children who so perfectly resemble God.

Against Such Things There Is No Law

Philippians 2:5

"Have this attitude in yourselves

which was also in Christ Jesus."

Chapter 7

Goodness

The fruit of goodness

Seeking goodness according to the desires of the Holy Spirit

Choose goodness in all things like the good Samaritan

Do not quarrel or boast in any situation

Do not break a battered reed or put out a smoldering wick

Power to follow goodness in the truth

Goodness

One night, a young man with shabby clothes went to see an elderly couple for a room for rent. The couple took pity on him and rented the room out to him. But this young man did not go to work, but just spent his days drinking. In a case such as this most people would want to put him out thinking that he might not be able to pay the rent. But this elderly couple gave him food from time to time and encouraged him while preaching the gospel. He was touched by their loving acts, because they were treating him as though he was their own son. He eventually accepted Jesus Christ and became a renewed man.

The fruit of goodness

To love even the neglected or social outcasts until the end without giving up on them is goodness. The fruit of goodness is not only borne in the heart but it is revealed in action as in the account of the elderly couple.

If we bear the fruit of goodness, we will give out the fragrance of the Christ everywhere. People around us will be touched seeing our good deeds and give glory to God.

"Goodness" is the quality of being gentle, considerate, kindhearted, and virtuous. In the spiritual sense, however, it is the heart that seeks goodness in the Holy Spirit, which is goodness in the truth. If we fully bear this fruit of goodness, we will have the Lord's heart that is pure and spotless.

Sometimes, even the unbelievers who have not received the Holy Spirit follow goodness in their lives to some extent. Worldly people discern and judge whether something is good or evil according to their consciences. In the absence of having pangs of conscience, worldly people think they are good and righteous. But a person's conscience is different from person to person. To understand goodness as in the fruit of the Spirit, we first have to understand people's conscience.

Seeking goodness according to the desires of the Holy Spirit

Some new believers might pass judgment on the sermons according to their own knowledge and conscience, saying, "That remark is not in agreement with this scientific theory." But as they grow up in faith and learn the Word of God, they come to realize that their standard of judgment is not correct.

Conscience is the standard to discern between good and evil, which is based on the foundation of one's nature. One's nature depends on the kind of life-energy one is born with and the kind of environment where he is raised. Those children who receive good life-energy have relatively good natures. Also, people who are raised in a good environment, seeing and hearing many good things, are likely to form good consciences. On the other hand, if one is born with many evil natures from his parents and comes in contact with many evil things, his nature and conscience are likely to become evil.

For example, children who are taught to be honest will have qualms of conscience when they tell a lie. But those children who are raised among liars will feel it is only natural to lie. They do not even think they are lying. In thinking that it is OK to lie, their consciences are stained with evil so much that they don't even have pangs of conscience about it.

Also, even though children are raised by the same parents in the same environment, they accept things in different ways. Some children just obey their parents while some other children have very strong wills and tend not to obey. Then, even though siblings are raised by the same parents, their consciences will be formed differently.

Consciences will form differently depending on the social and economic values where they grow up. Each society has a different value system, and the standard of 100 years ago, 50 years ago, and that of today are all different. For example, when they used to have slaves, they didn't think it was wrong to beat the slaves and force them to work. Also, just about 30 years ago, it was socially unacceptable for women to expose their bodies in public broadcasting. As mentioned, consciences become different according to individual, area, and time. Those who think they follow their conscience are merely following what they think is good. However, they cannot be said to act in absolute goodness.

But we who are believers in God have the same standard with which we distinguish between good and evil. We have the Word of God as the standard. This standard is the same yesterday, today, and forever. Spiritual goodness is to have this truth as our conscience and follow it. It is the willingness to follow the desires of the Holy Spirit and seek goodness. But just by having the desire to follow goodness, we cannot say we have borne the fruit of goodness. We can say we bear the fruit only when that desire to follow goodness is demonstrated and practiced in action.

Matthew 12:35 says, *"The good man brings out of his good treasure what is good."* Proverbs 22:11 also says, *"He who loves purity of heart and whose speech is gracious, the king is his friend."* As in the above verses, those who really seek goodness will naturally have good actions that can be seen externally. Wherever they go and whomever they meet, they show generosity and love with good words and deeds. Just like a person who sprayed perfume will give out a nice fragrance, those with goodness will give out the fragrance of Christ.

Some people long to cultivate a good heart, so they follow spiritual persons and want to have friendships with them. They enjoy hearing and learning the truth. They are easily touched and shed many tears, too. But they cannot cultivate a good heart just because they have the longing for it. If they heard and learned something, they have to cultivate it in their heart and actually practice it. For example, if you only like being around good people and avoid those who are not good, is it really longing for goodness?

There are also things to learn from even those who are not really good. Even though you cannot learn anything from them, you can receive a lesson from their lives. If there is somebody who has a hot temper, you can learn that by having a hot-temper he frequently gets into quarrels and arguments. From this observation you learn why you should not have such a temper. If you only keep company with those who are good, you cannot learn from the relativity of things that you see or hear. There are always things to learn from all kinds of people. You might think you are longing for goodness very much, and learn and realize many things, but you should check yourself as to whether you lack actual deeds of accumulating goodness.

Choose goodness in all things
like the good Samaritan

From this point on, let's look in more detail at what spiritual goodness is, which is to pursue goodness in the truth and in the Holy Spirit. In fact, spiritual goodness is a very broad concept. God's nature is goodness, and that goodness is embedded throughout the Bible. But a verse from which we can sense the aroma of goodness very well is from Philippians 2:1-4:

> *Therefore if there is any encouragement in Christ, if there is any consolation of love, if there is any fellowship of the Spirit, if any affection and compassion, make my joy complete by being of the same mind, maintaining the same love, united in spirit, intent on one purpose. Do nothing from selfishness or empty conceit, but with humility of mind regard one another as more important than yourselves; do not merely look out for your own personal interests, but also for the interests of others.*

A person who has borne spiritual goodness seeks goodness in the Lord, so he supports even the works that he doesn't really agree with. Such a person is humble and does not have any sense of vanity to be acknowledged or revealed. Even though others are not as wealthy or intelligent as he is, he can respect them from the heart and he can become their true friend.

Even though others give him a hard time without cause, he just accepts them with love. He serves them and humbles himself, so he can have peace with everybody. He would not only faithfully perform his duties but also care for other people's works. In Luke chapter 10, we have the parable of the Good Samaritan.

A man was robbed while travelling from Jerusalem to Jericho. The robbers stripped him and left him half dead. A priest was passing by and saw that he was dying, but that priest just passed by him. A Levite also saw him, but he also just passed by him as well. Priests and Levites are the ones who know the Word of God and who are serving God. They know the Law better than any of the people. They also take pride in how well they serve God.

When they had to follow the will of God they did not show the deeds that they were supposed to show. Of course, they could say they had reasons they couldn't help him. But if they had goodness, they couldn't just ignore a person who was in desperate need of their help.

Later, a Samaritan was passing by and saw this man who had been robbed. This Samaritan had pity on him and covered his wounds. He carried him on his animal and took him to an inn and asked the inn keeper to take care of him. Next day, he gave the inn keeper two denarii and promised that on his way back he would pay any additional costs the inn keeper incurred.

If the Samaritan had thought selfishly, he wouldn't have had any reason to do what he did. He too was busy, and he could suffer loss of time and money if he became involved in the affairs of a total stranger. Also, he could have just given him first aid, but he didn't have to ask the inn keeper to take care of him promising him that he would pay additional costs.

But because he had goodness, he couldn't just ignore a person who was dying. Even though he would suffer loss of time and money, and even though he was busy, he couldn't just overlook a person who was in desperate need of his help. When he couldn't help this person himself, he asked another person to help him. If he also had passed him by for his personal reasons as well, in the future this Samaritan would probably have had the burden of it on his heart.

He would have continuously questioned and blamed himself thinking, 'I wonder what happened to that man who was injured. I should have saved him even if I had to suffer loss. God was watching me and how could I have done that?' Spiritual goodness is being unable to bear with it if we do not choose the way of goodness. Even with the feeling that somebody is trying to deceive us, we choose goodness in all things.

Do not quarrel or boast in any situation

Another verse that lets us feel spiritual goodness is Matthew 12:19-20. Verse 19 says, *"He will not quarrel, nor cry out; nor will anyone hear His voice in the streets."* Next, verse 20 says, *"A battered reed He will not break off, and a smoldering wick He will not put out, until He leads justice to victory."*

This is about the spiritual goodness of Jesus. During His ministry, Jesus did not have any problems or quarrels with anybody. Since childhood He obeyed the Word of God, and during His public ministry, He did only good things, preaching the gospel of the kingdom of heaven and healing the sick. And yet, the evil ones tested Him with many words in an attempt to kill Him.

Every time, Jesus knew their evil intentions but did not hate them. He just let them realize the true will of God. When they could not realize it at all, He did not quarrel with them but just avoided them. Even when He was being questioned before the crucifixion, He did not quarrel or argue.

As we pass the stage of a novice in our Christian faith, we learn the Word of God to some extent. We would not readily raise our voice or throw a temper-tantrum just because of some disagreement with others. But quarreling is not just to raise our voice. If we have some uncomfortable feelings due to some disagreements, it is to have quarrel. We say it is a quarrel because the peace of the heart is broken.

If there is a quarrel in heart, the cause lies within oneself. It is not because somebody is giving us a hard time. It is not because they do not act in a way we think is right. It is because our hearts are too narrow to accept them, and it is because we have a framework of thoughts that puts us on a collision course with many things.

A piece of soft cotton would not make any noise when it is hit by any object. Even if we shake a glass that contains pure and clean water, that water will still remain pure and clean. It is the same with the heart of men. If the peace of mind is broken and some uncomfortable feelings come up in a certain situation, it is because evil is still present in the heart.

It is said Jesus did not cry out, so, for what reason do other people cry out? It is because they want to reveal and flaunt

Against Such Things There Is No Law

themselves. They cry out because they want to be recognized and served by other people.

Jesus manifested such tremendous works such as reviving the dead and opening the eyes of the blind. But, He was still humble. Furthermore, even when people were mocking Him while He was hung on the cross, He just obeyed the will of God until death, for He did not have any intention to reveal Himself (Philippians 2:5-8). It is also said nobody could hear His voice in the streets. It tells us His manners were perfect. He was perfect in His bearing, attitude, and way of speech. His extreme goodness, humbleness, and spiritual love that were deep inside His heart were revealed externally.

If we bear the fruit of spiritual goodness, we would not have any conflict or problems with anybody in the same way our Lord had no conflicts. We wouldn't speak of other people's faults or shortcomings. We wouldn't try to flaunt ourselves or to raise ourselves up among others. Even though we suffer unreasonably, we do not complain.

Do not break a battered reed or put out a smoldering wick

When we grow a tree or plants, if they have bruised leaves or branches, we will usually cut them off. Also, when a wick is smoldering, the light is not bright, and it gives out fumes and smoke. So, people just extinguish it. But those who have the spiritual goodness will not 'break a battered reed or put out a smoldering wick'. If there is the slightest bit of chance of recovery, they cannot cut that life off, and they try to open a way of life for others.

Here, the 'battered reed' refers to those who are filled with sins and evil of this world. The smoldering wick symbolizes those whose hearts are so stained with evil that the light of their soul is about to die out. It is unlikely that these people who are like battered reeds and smoldering wicks will accept the Lord. Even though they do believe in God, their deeds are no different from those of the worldly people. They even speak against the Holy Spirit or stand against God. At the time of Jesus, there were many who did not believe in Jesus. And even though they saw such amazing works of power, they still stood against the works of the Holy Spirit. Still, Jesus looked at them with faith until the end and opened opportunities for them to receive salvation.

Today, even in the churches, there are many people who are like battered reeds and smoldering wicks. They call, 'Lord, Lord' with their lips but still live in sins. Some of them even stand against God. With their weak faith, they stumble in temptation and stop attending church. After doing things that are recognized as evil in the church, they are so embarrassed that they leave the church. If we have goodness, we should first stretch out our hands to them.

Some people want to be loved and acknowledged in the church, but when it doesn't happen, the evil in them comes out. They become jealous of those who are loved by the church members and those who are advancing in spirit, and speak ill of them. They don't gather their heart for a certain work if it is not initiated by them, and they try to find fault with those works.

Even in these cases, those who have the fruit of spiritual goodness will accept these people who let their evil out. They don't try to distinguish who is right or wrong, or good or evil and then suppress them. They melt and touch their hearts by treating them in goodness with a truthful heart.

Some people ask me to reveal the identities of those people who attend the church with ulterior-motives. They say in doing so the church members will not be cheated and such people will not come to church at all. Yes, revealing their identities might purify the church, but how embarrassing would it be for their family members or those who brought them to the church? If we weed out church members for various reasons, not many people will remain in the church. It is one of the duties of a church to change even evil people and to lead them to the kingdom of heaven.

Of course, some people continue to show increasing evil, and they will fall into the way of death even though we show goodness to them. But even in these cases, we will not just set a limit of our endurance and forsake them if they go over that limit. It is the spiritual goodness to try to allow them to seek spiritual life without giving up until the end.

The wheat and the chaff look similar but the chaff is empty inside. After the harvest, the farmer will gather the wheat into the barn and burn the chaff. Or he will use it as fertilizer. There are the wheat and the chaff in the church, too. On the outside, everyone might look like they are believers, but there is the wheat that obeys the Word of God while there is the chaff that follows evil.

But just as the farmer waits until the harvest, God of love waits

Goodness

for those who are like chaff to change until the end. Until the final day comes, we have to give chances for everyone to be saved and look at everyone with the eyes of faith, by cultivating spiritual goodness in us.

Power to follow goodness in the truth

You might be confused as to how this spiritual goodness is differentiated from other spiritual characteristics. Namely, in the parable of the Good Samaritan, his acts can be described as charitable in mind and merciful; and if we do not quarrel or raise our voices, then we must be at peace and in humbleness. Then, are all these things included in the character of spiritual goodness?

Of course, love, charitableness of heart, mercy, peace, and humbleness all belong within goodness. As mentioned previously, goodness is the nature of God and it is a very broad concept. But the distinctive aspects of spiritual goodness are the desire to follow such goodness and the strength to actually practice it. The focus is not on mercy of having pity on others or the acts of helping them itself. The focus is on the goodness with which the Samaritan couldn't just pass by when he was supposed to have mercy.

Also, not quarreling and not speaking out is a part of being humble. But the character of spiritual goodness in these cases is that we cannot break peace because we follow spiritual goodness. Rather than crying out and being recognized, we want to be humble because we follow this goodness.

When being faithful, if you have the fruit of goodness, you will be faithful in not only one thing but also in all God's households. If you neglect any of your duties, there might be somebody who suffers because of it. God's kingdom might not be accomplished as it should be. So, if you have goodness in you, you will not feel comfortable about these things. You cannot just neglect them, so you will try to be faithful in all God's house. You can apply this principle to all other characters of spirit.

Those who are evil will be uncomfortable if they do not act out in evil. To the extent that they have evil, they will feel OK only after giving out that much evil. For those who have the habit of cutting in while others are talking, they cannot control themselves if they cannot interfere with other people's conversations. Even though they hurt others' feelings or give hard times to them, they can be at peace with themselves only after doing what they want. Nevertheless, if they remember and keep on trying to cast away their bad habits and attitudes that are not in agreement with the Word of God, they will be able to cast away most of them. But if they do not try and just give up, they will remain the same even after ten or twenty years.

But the men of goodness are the opposite. If they do not follow goodness, they will have more uncomfortable feelings than when they suffer a loss, and they will think about it repeatedly. So, even though they suffer some loss, they do not want to harm others. Even though they find it inconvenient, they try to keep the rules.

We can feel this heart from what Paul said. He had the faith to eat meat, but if it could cause any other person to stumble, he didn't want to eat any meat for the remainder of his life. In the same way, if what they can enjoy might cause any kind of discomfort to others, people of goodness would rather not enjoy it and find it happier to give it up for the sake of others. They could not do anything that would embarrass others; and, they could never do something that would make the Holy Spirit in them groan.

Likewise, if you follow goodness in all things, it means you are bearing the fruit of spiritual goodness. If you bear the fruit of spiritual goodness, you will have the attitude of the Lord. You will not do anything that can make even a little one stumble. You will have goodness and humbleness on the outside as well. You will be respectable having the form of the Lord, and your behavior and language will all be perfect. You will be beautiful in everyone's sight, giving out the fragrance of Christ.

Matthew 5:15-16 says, "...nor does anyone light a lamp and put it under a basket, but on the lampstand, and it gives light to all who are in the house. Let your light shine before men in such a way that they may see your good works, and glorify your Father who is in heaven." Also, 2 Corinthians 2:15 says, "For we are a fragrance of Christ to God among those who are being saved and among those who are perishing." Therefore, I hope you will give glory to God in all things by bearing the fruit of spiritual goodness quickly and giving out the aroma of Christ to the world.

Numbers 12:7-8

"He is faithful in all My household;

With him I speak mouth to mouth, even openly,

And not in dark sayings,

And he beholds the form of the LORD."

Chapter 8

Faithfulness

For our faithfulness to be recognized
Do more than the work given
Be faithful in the truth
Work according to the master's will.
Be faithful in all God's household
Faithfulness for God's kingdom and righteousness

Faithfulness

A man was going on a trip to a foreign country. While away his assets needed to be taken care of, so he gave this job to his three servants. According to their capability he gave each one talent, two talents, and five talents respectively. The servant who received five talents conducted merchandising for his master and gained an additional five talents. The servant given two talents also gained two more talents. But the one with one talent just buried the talent in the ground and did not make any profit.

The master praised the servants who earned the two and five additional talents and gave them rewards, saying *"Well done, good and faithful slave"* (Matthew 25:21). But he rebuked the servant who just buried the one talent saying, *"You wicked and lazy slave"* (v. 26).

God also gives us many duties according to our talents, so we can work for Him. Only when we fulfill the duties with all our strength and benefit the kingdom of God, can we be recognized as a 'good and faithful servant'.

For our faithfulness to be recognized

The dictionary definition of the word 'faithfulness' is 'the quality of being steadfast in affection or allegiance, or firm in adherence to promises or in observance of duty'. Even in the world, faithful people are valued highly for being trustworthy.

But the kind of faithfulness that is recognized by God is different from that of the worldly people. Just fulfilling our duty completely in action cannot be spiritual faithfulness. Also, if we put all our effort and even our lives in one particular area, it is not complete faithfulness. If we fulfill our duties as a wife, a mother, or a husband, can it be called faithfulness? It is only that we did what we had to do.

Those who are spiritually faithful are treasures in the kingdom of God and they give out a fragrant aroma. They give out the fragrance of an unchanging heart, the fragrance of steadfast obedience. One might compare it to the obedience of a good work cow and the fragrance of a trustworthy heart. If we can give out these kinds of fragrances, the Lord will also say we are so lovely and He wants to embrace us. It was the case with Moses.

The sons of Israel had been slaves in Egypt for more than 400 years, and Moses had the duty to lead them to the land of Canaan. He was so loved by God that God talked to him face to face. He was faithful in all God's household and fulfilled everything God commanded of him. He did not even consider all the problems he might have to undertake. He was much more than faithful in all areas in fulfilling the duty of the leader of Israel as well as being faithful to his family.

One day, Moses' father-in-law, Jethro, came to him. Moses talked to him about all the amazing things that God had done for the people of Israel. The next day, Jethro saw something strange. The people lined up beginning early in the morning to see Moses. They brought to Moses the disputes they could not judge among themselves. Jethro now made a suggestion.

Exodus 18:21-22 says, *"Furthermore, you shall select out of all the people able men who fear God, men of truth, those who hate dishonest gain; and you shall place these over them as leaders of thousands, of hundreds, of fifties and of tens. Let*

Against Such Things There Is No Law

them judge the people at all times; and let it be that every major dispute they will bring to you, but every minor dispute they themselves will judge. So it will be easier for you, and they will bear the burden with you."

Moses listened to his words. He realized his father-in-law had a point and accepted his suggestion. Moses selected able men who hated dishonest gain and placed them over the people as leaders of thousands, of hundreds, of fifties and of tens. They acted as judges for the people in routine and simpler matters and Moses judged only major disputes.

One can bear the fruit of faithfulness when he fulfills all his duties with a good heart. Moses was faithful to his family members as well as serving the people. He expended all his time and effort, and for this reason he was recognized as one who is faithful in all God's household. Numbers 12:7-8 says, *"Not so, with My servant Moses, he is faithful in all My household; with him I speak mouth to mouth, even openly, and not in dark sayings, and he beholds the form of the LORD."*

Now, what kind of person is one who has borne the fruit of faithfulness recognized by God?

Do more than the work given

When workers are paid for their work, we don't say they are faithful when they just fulfill their duties. We can say they did their job, but they did only what they are paid for, so we cannot

123

say they are faithful. But even among the paid workers, there are some who do more than what they are paid for to do. They don't do it with reluctance or just thinking they have to do at least as much as they are paid. They fulfill the duty with all their heart, mind, and soul, without sparing their time and money, having the desire coming from the heart.

Some of the full-time church workers do more than what is given to them. They work after working hours or on holidays, and when they are not working, they always think about their duty for God. They always think of the ways to better serve the church and the members by doing more than the job given to them. Moreover, they assume the duties of cell group leaders to take care of the souls. It is in this way that it is faithfulness to do much more than what is entrusted to us.

Also, in taking responsibility, those who bear the fruit of faithfulness will do more than what they are responsible for doing. For example, in the case of Moses, he put up his life when he prayed to save the sons of Israel who had committed sins. We can see this from his prayer found in Exodus 32:31-32, which says, *"Alas, this people has committed a great sin, and they have made a god of gold for themselves. But now, if You will, forgive their sin and if not, please blot me out from Your book which You have written!"*

When Moses was fulfilling this duty, he did not just obey in action to do what God commanded him to do. He did not think, 'I did my best in delivering the will of God to them, but they didn't accept it. I can't help them anymore.' He had the heart of God and guided the people with all his love and effort. That is why, when the people committed sins, he felt as if it were his own fault, and he wanted to take the responsibility for it.

It is the same with the apostle Paul. Romans 9:3 says, *"For I could wish that I myself were accursed, separated from Christ for the sake of my brethren, my kinsmen according to the flesh,"* But even though we hear and know about Paul's and Moses' faithfulness, it does not necessarily mean we have cultivated faithfulness.

Even those who have faith and perform their duties would have something different to say than what Moses said if they were in the same situation that he had been. Namely, they might say, "God, I did my best. I feel pity for the people, but I have also suffered a lot while leading these people." What they are really saying is "I am confident because I did everything I was supposed to do." Or, they may worry that they will receive the rebuke together with others for those people's sins, even though they themselves were not responsible. The heart of such people as this is quite far from faithfulness.

Of course, not just anybody can pray, "Please forgive their sins or blot me out of the book of life." It just means that if we bear the fruit of faithfulness in our heart, we cannot just say we are not responsible for the things that went wrong. Before we think we did our best in our deeds, we would first think about the kind of heart we had when duties were given to us for the first time.

Also, we will first think of the love and mercy of God for the souls and that God does not want them to be destroyed even though He says He is going to punish them for their sins. Then, what kind of prayer would we offer to God? We would probably say from the depth of our hearts, "God, it is my fault. It was me who didn't guide them better. Give them one more chance in consideration of my behalf."

It's the same in all the other aspects. Those who are faithful will not just say, "I've done enough," but they will work overflowingly with all their heart. In 2 Corinthians 12:15 Paul said, *"I will most gladly spend and be expended for your souls. If I love you more, am I to be loved less?"*

Namely, Paul was not coerced to take care of the souls nor did he do it superficially. He took great joy in fulfilling his duty and that is why he said he would be expended for other souls.

He offered himself again and again with complete devotion for other souls. As in Paul's case, it is true faithfulness if we can fulfill our duty overflowingly with joy and love.

Be faithful in the truth

Suppose somebody joined a gang and dedicated his life to the boss of the gang. Will God say he is faithful? Of course not! God can recognize our faithfulness only when we are faithful in goodness and truth.

As Christians lead a diligent life in faith, they are likely to be given many duties. In some cases they try to fulfill their duties with fervor at first, but just give them up at a certain point. Their minds can be taken away by the business expansion they are planning. They might lose their fervor for their duty because of difficulties in life or because they want to avoid persecutions from others. Why does their mind change this way? It is because they

126

neglected spiritual faithfulness while working for God's kingdom.

Spiritual faithfulness is to circumcise our heart. It is to wash the robe of our hearts continually. It is to cast away all kinds of sins, untruths, evil, unrighteousness, lawlessness, and darkness and become holy. Revelation 2:10 says, *"Be faithful until death, and I will give you the crown of life."* Here, to be faithful until death does not just mean we have to work hard and faithfully until our physical death. It also means we have to try to accomplish the Word of God in the Bible fully with all our lives.

In order to accomplish spiritual faithfulness, we first have to struggle against sins to the point of shedding blood and keep the commandments of God. The top priority is to cast away evil, sin, and untruths that God hates very much. If we are just physically working hard without circumcising our heart, we do not say it is spiritual faithfulness. As Paul said "I die daily," we have to put our flesh to death completely and become sanctified. This is spiritual faithfulness.

What God the Father desires of us the most is holiness. We have to realize this point and do our best in circumcising our hearts. Of course, it doesn't mean we cannot assume any duties before we become completely sanctified. It means whatever duty we are carrying on right now, we have to accomplish holiness while fulfilling our duties.

Those who continuously circumcise their hearts will not have changes of attitude in their faithfulness. They will not give up their precious duty just because they have difficulties in everyday life or some afflictions of the heart. God-given duties are a promise made between God and us, and we must never break our promises with God in any hardships.

Faithfulness

On the other hand, what will happen if we neglect the circumcision of our hearts? We won't be able to keep our heart when we are faced with difficulties and hardships. We may forsake the relationship of trust with God and give up our duty. Then, if we recover the grace of God, we work hard again for a while, and this cycle goes on and on. Those workers who have fluctuations like this cannot be recognized to be faithful, even though they may do their jobs well.

To have the faithfulness acknowledged by God, we must have the spiritual faithfulness as well, which means we have to circumcise our hearts. But circumcising our heart in itself does not become our rewards. Circumcising the heart is a must for children of God who are saved. But if we cast away sins and fulfill our duties with a sanctified heart, we can bear much greater fruit than when we fulfill them with fleshly minds. Therefore, we will receive much greater rewards.

For example, suppose you sweat while volunteering in the church all day on Sunday. But you had quarrels with many other people and you broke peace with many people. If you serve the church while complaining and have resentment, so much of your rewards will be subtracted. But if you serve the church with goodness and love being at peace with others, all your work will be an aroma acceptable to God, and each of your deeds will become your reward.

Work according to the master's will

In the church, we have to work according to the heart and will of God. Also, we have to be faithful obeying our leaders according to the order within the church. Proverbs 25:13 says, *"Like the cold of snow in the time of harvest is a faithful messenger to those who send him, for he refreshes the soul of his masters."*

Even though we are very diligent in our duty, we cannot quench the desire of the master if we just do what we want. For example, suppose your boss in your company tells you to remain in the office because a very important customer is coming. But you have some office-related business outside and you take care of the matter, but it takes all day long. Even if you are out for office work, in the eyes of the boss you are not faithful.

The reason why we do not obey the master's will is either because we follow our own ideas or because we have self-centered motives. This kind of person may seem to be serving his master, but he is not actually doing it with faithfulness. He is only following his own thoughts and desires, and he has shown that he can forsake the master's will at any time.

In the Bible we read about a person named Joab, who was a relative and the general of the army of David. Joab was with David through all the dangers while David was being chased by King Saul. He had wisdom and he was valiant. He managed the things that David wanted to be done. When he attacked the Ammonites and took their city, he practically conquered it, but he let David come and take it himself. He did not take the glory of conquering the city but let David take it.

He served David so very well this way, but David was not very comfortable with him. It was because he disobeyed David when it was personally beneficial for him. Joab did not hesitate to act insolently before David when he wanted to achieve his goal.

For example, general Abner, who was an enemy of David, came to David surrendering to him. David welcomed him and sent him back. It was because David could stabilize the people more quickly by accepting him. But when Joab found out this fact later, he followed Abner and killed him. It was because Abner had killed Joab's brother in a previous battle. He knew David would be in a difficult situation if he killed Abner, but he just followed his emotions.

Also, when David's son Absalom rebelled against David, David asked the soldiers who were going to fight with the men of Absalom to treat his son with kindness. Having heard this order, Joab still just killed Absalom. Maybe it was because if they let Absalom live, he could have rebelled again, but in the end, Joab disobeyed the king's order at his own discretion.

Even though he went through all the difficult times with the king, he disobeyed the king at crucial moments, and David could not trust him. Finally, Joab rebelled against King Solomon, David's son, and was put to death. At this time too, rather than obeying the will of David, he wanted to install the person whom he thought should be the king. He served David throughout all his life, but instead of becoming a meritorious retainer, his life ended as a rebel.

When we do God's work, rather than how ambitiously we do the work, the more important factor is whether we are following the will of God. It is of no use to be faithful going against the will of God. When we work in the church, we should also follow our leaders before we follow our own ideas. This way, the enemy devil and Satan cannot bring any accusations and we will all be able to give glory to God in the end.

Be faithful in all God's household

'To be faithful in all God's household' means to be faithful in all aspects related to ourselves. In the church, we have to fulfill all our responsibilities even when we have many duties. Even though we don't have a particular duty in the church, it is one of our duties to be present where we are supposed to be present as a member.

Not only in the church, but in places of work and school, everyone has his duties. In all these aspects, we have to fulfill our duties as the members. To be faithful in all God's household is to fulfill all our duties in all respects of our lives: as God's children, as leaders or members of the church, as members of the family, as employees in the company, or as students or teachers in school. We should not just be faithful only in one or two duties and neglect other duties. We have to be faithful in all aspects.

One might think, 'I have only one body and how can I be faithful in all the areas?' But to the extent that we change into spirit, it is not something difficult to be faithful in all God's household. Even though we invest just a little time, we can surely reap the fruit if we sow in spirit.

Also, those who have changed into spirit do not follow their own benefit and comfort but think about others' benefit. They view things from the stand-point of others first. Thus, such people will take care of all their duties even if they must sacrifice themselves. Also, to the extent to which we attain to the level of

131

spirit, our heart will be filled with goodness. And if we are good we will not incline towards only one particular side. So, even if we have many duties, we will not neglect any of the duties.

We will do our best to take care of all our surroundings, trying to care for others a little more. Then, people around us will feel the truthfulness of our heart. So, they will not be disappointed because we cannot be with them all the time but they will rather be thankful that we care for them.

For example, one person has two duties, and she is the leader in one of the groups and just a member in the other. Here, if she has goodness and if she bears the fruit of faithfulness, she will not neglect either one of them. She will not just say, "the members of the latter group will understand me for not being with them because I am the leader of the former group." If she cannot be physically be with the latter group, she will try to be some kind of help to that group in other ways and in the heart. Likewise, we can be faithful in all God's household and have peace with everybody to the extent that we have goodness.

Faithfulness for God's kingdom and righteousness

Joseph was sold as a slave into the house of Potiphar, the captain of the royal bodyguard. And Joseph was so faithful and trustworthy that Potiphar left all of the work in the house with this young slave and did not care about what he did. It was because Joseph took care of even little things with all his best, having the heart of the master.

The kingdom of God also needs many faithful workers like Joseph in many areas. If you have a certain duty, and you fulfill it so faithfully that your leader doesn't have to look after it at all, then, how great a strength you will be for the kingdom of God!

Luke 16:10 says, *"He who is faithful in a very little thing is faithful also in much; and he who is unrighteous in a very little thing is unrighteous also in much."* Though he served a physical master, Joseph worked faithfully with his faith in God. God did not take it to be meaningless, but instead He made Joseph the prime minister of Egypt.

I have never been at ease about the works of God. I always offered all-night prayers even before opening of the church, but after the church opened, I prayed from the midnight until 4 AM personally and then led the dawn prayer meetings at 5 AM. At that time we did not have the Daniel prayer meeting that we have today, starting at 9 PM. We did not have any other pastors or cell leaders, so I had to lead all the dawn prayer meetings all by myself. But I never missed a day.

Furthermore, I had to prepare the sermons for the Sunday services, Wednesday services, and Friday all-night services, while attending the theological seminary. I never pushed my duties off and on to others just because I was tired. After I came back from the seminary, I took care of the sick people or made visitations to the members. There were so many sick people who came from all over the country. I put in all my heart each time I made a visitation to a church member to spiritually serve them.

At that time, some of the students had to take the bus with

Faithfulness

two or three changes to come to the church. Now, we have buses in the church, but at that time we didn't. So, I wanted the students to be able to come to the church without having to worry about the bus fares. I followed the students after worship services to the bus stop and gave them the bus tokens or tickets seeing them off. I gave them enough bus tokens so they had enough to come to the church next time, too. The amount of offerings for the church was only about several tens of dollars, and it could not be taken care of by the church. I gave them the bus fares with my own savings.

When a new person registered, I considered each of them as a precious treasure, so I prayed for them and served them with love not to lose any of them. For this reason at that time none of the people who registered in the church left. Naturally, the church kept on growing. Now that the church has many members, does that mean my faithfulness has cooled down? Of course not! My fervor for the souls has never cooled down.

Now, we have more than 10,000 branch churches worldwide as well as so many pastors, elders, senior deaconesses, and leaders for districts, sub-districts, and cell groups. And yet, my prayers and love for the souls have only been growing more fervently.

By any chance has your faithfulness before God cooled down? Is there anyone among you who used to have God-given duties, but no longer have any duties now? If you have the same duty now as in the past, hasn't your fervor for the duty cooled down? If we have true faith, our faithfulness will only increase as we mature in our faith, and we are faithful in the Lord to accomplish the kingdom of God and to save numerous souls. So, we will receive a great deal in precious rewards later in Heaven!

If God wanted faithfulness only in deeds, He did not have to create the mankind, because there are countless heavenly host and angels who obey very well. But God did not want somebody who obeys unconditionally, somewhat like robots. He wanted children who would be faithful with their love for God stemming from the depth of their hearts.

Psalm 101:6 says, *"My eyes shall be upon the faithful of the land, that they may dwell with me; he who walks in a blameless way is the one who will minister to me."* Those who cast away all forms of evil and become faithful in all God's household will receive the blessing to enter into New Jerusalem, which is the most beautiful dwelling place in Heaven. Therefore, I hope you will become workers who are like pillars of the kingdom of God and enjoy the honor of staying close to the throne of God.

Matthew 11:29

"Take My yoke upon you and learn from Me,

for I am gentle and humble in heart,

and you will find rest for your souls."

Chapter 9

Gentleness

Gentleness

Surprisingly many people worry about hot-temperedness, depression, or about their characters that are extremely introversive or too extroversive. Some people just attribute everything to their personalities when things do not go as they want, saying, "I cannot help it, it is my personality." But God created men, and it is not difficult for God to change the personalities of men with His power.

Moses once killed another man due to his temper, but he was changed by the power of God to such an extent that he was acknowledged by God to be the most humble and meekest person on the face of the earth. The apostle John had the nickname, 'son of thunder', but he was changed by the power of God and was acknowledged as 'the gentle apostle'.

If they are willing to cast away evil and plow their heart-fields, even those who have hot-tempers, those who brag, and those who are self-centered can be changed and cultivate characters of gentleness.

Gentleness to accept many people

In the dictionary gentleness is the quality or state of being gentle, soft, tender, or mild. Those who are timid or 'shyly non-social' in character, or those who cannot express themselves very well may appear to be gentle. Those who are naïve or those who don't get angry at all due to low intellectual level may appear to be gentle in the eyes of the worldly people.

But spiritual gentleness is not simply mildness and soft tenderness. It is to have wisdom and the ability to discern between

Gentleness

the right and wrong, and at the same time to be able to understand and accept everybody because in them there is no evil. Namely, spiritual gentleness is to have generosity coupled with a mild and soft character. If you have this virtuous generosity, you won't just be mild all the time, but you also have stern dignity when necessary.

The heart of the gentle person is as soft as cotton. If you throw a stone at cotton or poke it with a needle, the cotton will just cover and embrace the object. Likewise, no matter how other people treat them, those who are spiritually gentle will not have hard feelings in their hearts toward them. Namely, they don't get angry or experience discomfort, and they do not cause discomfort for others, either.

They do not pass judgment or condemnation but are understanding and accepting. People will feel comfort from such people, and many people are able to come and find rest in those who are gentle. It's just like a big tree with many branches to which birds can come, nest and rest on the branches.

Moses is one of the persons who was acknowledged by God for his gentleness. Numbers 12:3 says, *"Now the man Moses was very humble, more than any man who was on the face of the earth."* At the time of the Exodus the number of the sons of Israel was more than 600,000 adult men. Including women and children it would have been much more than two million. Leading such a vast number of people in itself would be a very difficult task for an ordinary person.

It is especially so for these people who had hardened hearts as former slaves of Egypt. If you are regularly beaten, hear foul and abusive language, and do the laborious work of slaves, your heart would become rough and hardened. In this condition, it is not easy to engrave any grace in their hearts or for them to be able to love God from the heart. That is why the people disobeyed God every time even though Moses showed them such great power.

When faced with just a little bit of difficulty in their situations, they soon began to complain and stood against Moses. Just by seeing the fact that Moses led such people in the wilderness for 40 years, we can understand how spiritually gentle Moses was. This heart of Moses is spiritual gentleness, which is one of the fruits of the Holy Spirit.

Spiritual gentleness accompanied by generosity

But is there anybody who thinks something like the following, 'I don't get angry, and I think I am gentler than others, but I don't really receive answers to my prayer. I don't really hear the voice of the Holy Spirit very well either'? Then, you should check whether or not your gentleness is fleshly gentleness. People might say you are gentle if you appear to be mild and calm, but it is only fleshly gentleness.

What God wants is spiritual gentleness. Spiritual gentleness is not just to be gentle and mild but it has to be accompanied by virtuous generosity. Along with the meekness in heart, you should also have the quality of virtuous generosity visible on the outside in order to completely cultivate spiritual gentleness. It is much the same as a person with excellent character who is wearing a suit that matches his character. Even if a person has a good character, if he goes around naked without clothing, his nakedness will be to his shame. Likewise, gentleness without virtuous generosity is not complete.

Virtuous generosity is like the outfit that makes the gentleness shine, but it is different from legalistic or hypocritical acts. If holiness is not in your heart, it cannot be said that you have virtuous generosity just because you have good outward deeds. If you incline towards showing appropriate acts rather than cultivating your heart, you are likely to stop realizing your shortcomings and mistakenly think that you have accomplished spiritual growth to a great extent.

But even in this world, people who only have outward appearances without having good personalities will not gain the hearts of others. In faith, too, concentrating on the outward deeds without cultivating the inner beauty is meaningless.

For example, some people act uprightly, but they pass judgment and look down on others who don't act like them. They may also insist on their own standards when dealing with others thinking, 'This is the right way, so why don't they just do it this way?' They may speak nice words when they give advice, but they pass judgment on others in their hearts, and they speak within their self-righteousness and ill-feelings. People cannot find rest in these people. They will only be hurt and discouraged, so they wouldn't want to remain close to these people.

Some people also get angry and get irritated within their self-righteousness and evil. But they say they only have 'righteous indignation' and it is for the sake of others. But those who have virtuous generosity will not lose the peace of mind in any situation.

If you really want to bear the fruits of the Holy Spirit completely, you cannot just cover the evil in your heart with your outer appearances. If you do, then it is only a show for other people. You have to check yourself again and again in everything and choose the way of goodness.

Characteristics of those who have borne the fruit of gentleness

When people see those who are gentle and have broad hearts, they say these people's hearts are like an ocean. The ocean accepts all the polluted waters from streams and rivers and purifies them. If we cultivate a broad and gentle heart like the ocean, we can lead even sin-stained souls to the way of salvation.

If we have generosity on the outside along with gentleness inside, we can gain the hearts of many people, and we can accomplish many great things. Now, let me give you some examples of the characteristics of those who have borne the fruit of gentleness.

First, they are dignified and moderate in their actions.

Those who appear mild in temperament but are actually indecisive cannot accept others. They will be looked down upon and used by others. In history, some kings were gentle in character but did not have virtuous generosity, so the country was not stable. Later in history people evaluate him not as a gentle person but as being incapable and indecisive.

On the other hand, some kings had warm and mild characters along with wisdom accompanied by dignity. Under the rule of such kings, the country was stable and the people had peace. Likewise, those who have both gentleness and virtuous generosity have a proper standard of judgment. They do what is righteous by discerning the right and wrong correctly.

When Jesus purified the Temple and rebuked the hypocrisy of the Pharisees and the scribes, He was very strong and stern. He has a gentle heart so as not to 'break a bruised reed or put out a smoldering wick', but still He rebuked the people harshly when He had to. If you have such dignity and righteousness in heart, people cannot look down on you even though you never raise your voice or try to become stern.

Outward appearance is also related to possessing the manners of the Lord and the perfect deeds of the body. Those who are virtuous have dignity, authority and importance in their words; they don't carelessly speak meaningless words. They put on appropriate clothes for each occasion. They have mild facial expressions, but not brusque or cold faces.

For example, suppose a person has untidy hair and clothes, and his bearing is undignified. Suppose he also likes telling jokes and talks about meaningless things. It is probably very difficult for such a person to gain trust and respect from others. Other people would not want to be accepted and be embraced by him.

If Jesus had been jesting all the time, His disciples would have tried to joke with Him. So, if Jesus had taught them something difficult, they would have immediately argued or insisted on their own opinions. But they could not dare to do that. Even those who came to Him to argue could not really argue with Him because of His dignity. Jesus' words and actions always had weight and dignity, so the people could not just consider Him lightly.

Of course, sometimes the superior in hierarchy can make a joke to his subordinates in order to ease the mood. But if the subordinates jest together being ill-mannered, this means they do not have proper understanding. But if the leaders are not upright, and show distracted appearances, they cannot gain trust from others, either. Especially, high-ranking senior officers in a company must have upright attitudes, ways of speech, and behaviors.

A superior in organization might speak honorific language and act respectfully before his subordinates, but sometimes, if one of his subordinates is showing excessive respect, this superior might speak in ordinary language, not in honorific forms, in order to put his subordinate at ease. In this situation, not being too polite might rather make his subordinate feel at ease and he can open his heart more easily this way. But just because the superior is putting his subordinates at ease, the lower ranking people should not look down on their superiors, argue with them, or disobey them.

Romans 15:2 says, *"Each of us is to please his neighbor for his good, to his edification."* Philippians 4:8 says, *"Finally, brethren, whatever is true, whatever is honorable, whatever is right, whatever is pure, whatever is lovely, whatever is of good repute, if there is any excellence and if anything worthy of praise, dwell on these things."* Likewise, those who are virtuous and generous will do everything with uprightness, and they also have the consideration to make people feel comfortable.

Next, the gentle show actions of mercy and compassion having a broad heart.

They not only help those who are in financial need but also those who are spiritually weary and weak by comforting them and showing them grace. But even though they have gentleness in them, if that gentleness only stays in their heart, it is difficult to give out that fragrance of the Christ.

For example, suppose there is a believer who is suffering from persecutions for her faith. If the church leaders around her find it out, they feel compassion for her and pray for her. They are the leaders who feel compassion only in their hearts. On the other hand, some other leaders personally encourage and comfort her and also help her in deeds and action according to the situation. They strengthen her to help her overcome with faith.

So, just having the consideration in heart and showing the actual deeds will be very different for the person who is going through a problem. When the gentleness shows on the outside as generous deeds, it can give grace and life to others. Therefore, when the Bible says 'the gentle will inherit the earth' (Matthew 5:5), it has a close relationship with faithfulness that shows as a result of virtuous generosity. To inherit the earth is related to heavenly rewards. Usually, receiving heavenly rewards has a relationship with faithfulness. When you receive a plaque of appreciation, merit of honor, or an award for evangelism from the church, it is a result of your faithfulness.

Likewise, the gentle will receive blessings, but it doesn't just come from the gentle heart itself. When that gentle heart is expressed with virtuous and generous deeds, they will bear the

146

fruit of faithfulness. They then receive rewards as a result of it. Namely, when you accept and embrace many souls with generosity, comfort them and encourage them and give them life, you will inherit the earth in Heaven through such deeds.

To bear the fruit of gentleness

Now, how can we bear the fruit of gentleness? Conclusively speaking, we should cultivate our heart into a good soil.

And He spoke many things to them in parables, saying, "Behold, the sower went out to sow; and as he sowed, some seeds fell beside the road, and the birds came and ate them up. Others fell on the rocky places, where they did not have much soil; and immediately they sprang up, because they had no depth of soil. But when the sun had risen, they were scorched; and because they had no root, they withered away. Others fell among the thorns, and the thorns came up and choked them out. And others fell on the good soil and yielded a crop, some a hundredfold, some sixty, and some thirty" (Matthew 13:3-8).

In Matthew chapter 13, our heart is likened to four different kinds of soils. It can be categorized into the roadside, the rocky field, the thorny field, and good soil.

The heart soil that is likened to the roadside has to be broken of its self-righteousness and self-centered frameworks

The roadside is stepped on by people and is hardened, so seeds cannot be sown in it. The seeds cannot take root and are eaten up by the birds. Those who have such hearts have stubborn minds. They do not open their heart to the truth, so they cannot meet God nor posses faith.

Their own knowledge and value systems have been so very strongly firmed that they cannot accept the Word of God. They strongly believe they are right. In order for them to break down their self-righteousness and frameworks, they have to demolish the evil in their heart first. It is difficult to break down self-righteousness and frameworks if one keeps pride, arrogance, stubbornness, and falsehoods. Such evilness will cause the person to have fleshly thoughts that keep them from believing the Word of God.

For example, those who have been accumulating falsehoods in their minds cannot keep from doubting even if others are telling the truth. Romans 8:7 says, *"because the mind set on the flesh is hostile toward God; for it does not subject itself to the law of God, for it is not even able to do so."* As written, they cannot say 'Amen' to the Word of God nor obey it.

Some people are very stubborn in the beginning, but once they receive the grace and their thoughts are changed, they become very fervent in their faith. This is the case where they have hardened outer minds but soft and gentle inner hearts. But roadside-like people are different from these people. Theirs is the

Against Such Things There Is No Law

case where their inner hearts are also hardened. A heart that is hardened on the outside but gentle inside can be likened to a thin sheet of ice while the roadside can be likened to a pool of water that is frozen to the bottom.

Because the roadside-like heart has been hardened with untruths and evil for a long time, it is not easy to break it down in a short period of time. One has to keep on breaking it up again and again to cultivate it. Whenever the Word of God does not agree with their thoughts, they have to think as to whether their thoughts are really correct. Also, they have to store up deeds of goodness so that God can give them grace.

Sometimes, some people ask me to pray for them so that they can have faith. Of course, it's a pity that they cannot have faith even after witnessing the power of God and listening to the Word of God so much, but it is still much better than not trying at all. In the case of roadside-like hearts, their family members and church leaders have to pray for them and lead them, but it's important that they too have their own efforts. Then, at a certain point in time, the seed of the Word will begin to sprout in their hearts.

The heart likened to a rocky field has to cast away love for the world

If you sow seeds in a rocky field, they will sprout but cannot grow well due to the rocks. In the same way, those who have the heart of the rocky field soon fall when trials, persecutions, or temptations come.

When they receive God's grace, they feel like they really want to try to live by the Word of God. They might even experience fiery works of the Holy Spirit, too. That is to say, the seed of the Word fell on their heart and it sprang up. However, even after receiving this grace, they have conflicting thoughts arise when they are about to go to church the following Sunday. They certainly experienced the Holy Spirit, but they begin to doubt feeling that it was some kind of moment of emotional excitement. They have thoughts that make them doubt, and they close the door of their heart again.

For others the conflict might be that they cannot really quit their hobbies or other entertainments they are accustomed to enjoying, and they do not keep the Lord's Day. If they are persecuted by their family members or their bosses at work while they lead a Spirit-filled life in faith, they stop attending church. They greatly receive grace and seem to lead an ardent life in faith for some time, but if they have a problem with other believers in the church, they may be offended and they soon leave the church.

Then, what is the reason why the seed of the Word does not take root? It's because of the 'rocks' that are placed in the heart. The flesh of the heart is symbolically represented by 'rocks' and it is these untruths that keep them from obeying the Word. Among the many untruthful things, these are the ones that are so hard that they stop the seed of the Word from taking root. More specifically, it is the flesh of the heart that loves this world.

If they love some form of worldly entertainment, it's difficult for them to keep the Word telling them, "Keep the Sabbath holy." Also, those who have the rock of greed in their heart do not come to church because they hate giving the tithe and offerings to God.

Against Such Things There Is No Law

Some people have the rocks of hatred in their hearts, so the word of love cannot take root.

Among those who are attending church well, there are some who have the heart of the rocky field. For example, even though they were born and raised in Christian families and they learned the Word from childhood, they do not live by the Word. They experienced the Holy Spirit and sometimes received grace too, but they do not cast away their love for the world. While they are listening to the Word, they think to themselves that they shouldn't live like they are living now, but when they go back home they go back to the world again. They live their lives straddling the fence with one foot on the side of God and the other foot on the side of the world. Because of the Word they heard they do not leave God, but they still have many rocks in their heart that hinder the Word of God from taking root.

Also, some rocky fields are only partially rocky. For example, some people are faithful without any changing of mind. They also bear some fruits. But they have hatred in heart, and they have conflicts with others in every matter. They also pass judgment and condemnation, thus breaking peace everywhere. For this reason, after so many years, they do not bear the fruit of love or fruit of meekness. Others have gentle and good hearts. They are considerate and understanding of others, but they are not faithful. They easily break promises and are irresponsible in many aspects. So, they have to improve their shortcomings to plow their heart-field into good soil.

Now, what do we have to do to plow the rocky field?

Gentleness

First, we have to diligently follow the Word. A certain believer tries to fulfill his duties in obedience to the Word that tells us to be faithful. But it is not as easy as he thought.

When he was just a layman member of the church who didn't have a title or position, other members served him. But now in his position he has to serve other lay members. He may be trying hard, but he has hard feelings when he works with somebody who does not really agree with his ways. His ill-feelings such as resentment and hot-temper come up from his heart. He gradually loses the fullness of the Spirit, and he even thinks of quitting his duty.

Then, these ill-feelings are the rocks that he has to cast away from his heart-field. These ill-feelings are derived from the big rock called 'hatred'. When he tries to obey the Word, 'be faithful', he now faces the rock called 'hatred'. When he discovers it, he has to attack this rock called 'hatred' and pull it out. Only then can he obey the Word telling us to love and have peace. Also, he must not just give up only because it's hard, but he has to hold on to his duty even more firmly and fulfill it more passionately. This way, he can change into a worker who is gentle.

Secondly, we have to pray earnestly while practicing the Word of God. When the rain falls on the field, it will become moist and soft. It is a good time to remove the rocks. Likewise, when we pray, we will be filled with the Spirit, and our heart will become soft. When we are filled with the Holy Spirit by prayers, we should not miss that chance. We have to quickly take out the rocks. Namely, we have to immediately put the things into practice that we couldn't really obey before. As we keep on doing this again and again, even the big rocks placed deep inside can be shaken loose and pulled out. When we receive the grace and strength God has given from above and receive the fullness of the Holy Spirit, then we can cast away sins and evil that we could not cast away with our own willpower.

The thorny field does not bear fruit due to worries of the world and the deceitfulness of riches

If we sow seeds in thorny places, they may sprout and grow up, but due to the thorns they cannot bear any fruit. Likewise, those who have the heart like thorny fields believe and try to practice the Word that is given, but they cannot put the Word completely into practice. It's because they have worries of the world, and deceitfulness of riches, which is the greed for money, fame, and power. For this reason, they live in afflictions and trials.

Such people have constant worries of physical things such as house chores, their businesses, or their work tomorrow even though they come to church. They are supposed to gain comfort and new strength while attending the service in the church, but they only have mounting worries and concerns. Then, even though they spend so many Sundays in the church, they cannot taste the true joy and peace of keeping Sundays holy. If they truly kept Sundays holy, their souls would prosper and they would receive spiritual and material blessings. But, they are not able to receive such blessings. So, they have to remove the thorns and practice the Word of God properly so that they can have good heart-soil.

Now, how can we plow the thorny field?
We have to pull out the thorns at the root. Thorns symbolize

Gentleness

fleshly thoughts. Their roots symbolize evil and fleshly things of the heart. Namely, the evil and fleshly attributes in the heart are the sources of fleshly thoughts. If the branches are just cut off from the thorn bushes, they will grow again. Likewise, even though we make up our mind not to have fleshly thoughts, we cannot stop them as long as we have evil in our hearts. We have to pull out the flesh of the heart from the root.

Among the many roots, if we pull out the roots called greed and arrogance, we can cast away flesh from our heart to a significant extent. We are apt to be bound by the world and worry about worldly things because we have greed for fleshly things. Then we always think of what is self-beneficial and follow our own way, even though we may say we are living by the Word of God. Also, if we have arrogance we cannot obey completely either. We utilize fleshly wisdom and our fleshly thoughts because we think we are capable of doing something. Therefore, we first have to pull out the roots called greed and arrogance.

Cultivate good soil

When seeds are sown in good soil, they sprout and grow up to bear fruits 30, 60, or 100 times more. Those who have such heart-fields do not have self-righteousness and frameworks like those who have roadside-like hearts. They do not have any rocks or thorns, and thus they obey the Word of God with only 'Yes' and 'Amen'. This way, they can bear abundant fruit.

Of course, it is difficult to make clear distinctions between the roadside, rocky field, thorny field, and good soil of men's heart as if we were analyzing it with some measure. A roadside heart may contain some rocky soil. Even good soil can input some untruths that are like rocks in the growing process. But no matter what kind of field, we can make it good soil if we diligently plow it. Similarly, the important thing is how diligently we are plowing the field rather than what kind of heart-field we have.

Even a very rough barren land can be cultivated into a field of good soil if the farmer plows it very diligently. Likewise, the heart-fields of men can be changed by the power of God. Even the hardened hearts like the roadside can be plowed with the help of the Holy Spirit.

Of course, receiving the Holy Spirit does not necessarily mean our hearts will change automatically. There must be our own effort, too. We have to try to pray fervently, try to think only in the truth in everything, and try to practice the truth. We must not give up after trying several weeks or even several months, but we have to keep on trying.

God considers our effort before He gives us His grace and power and the help of the Holy Spirit. If we keep in mind what we have to change and actually change these characters by the grace and power of God and the help of the Holy Spirit, then we will definitely become very different after a year. We will speak good words following the truth, and our thoughts will change into good thoughts that are of the truth.

To the extent that we plow our heart-field into good soil, other fruits of the Holy Spirit will also be borne in us. In particular, gentleness is closely related to the cultivation of our heart-field. Unless we pull out various untruths such as temper, hatred, envy, greed, quarrels, boasting, and self-righteousness, we cannot have

Gentleness

gentleness. Then, other souls cannot find rest in us.

For this reason gentleness is more directly related with holiness than other fruits of the Holy Spirit. We can quickly receive anything we ask for in prayer like good soil that produces fruit, if we cultivate spiritual gentleness. We will also be able to hear the voice of the Holy Spirit clearly, so that we can be guided to prosperous ways in all things.

Blessings for the gentle

It is not easy to run a company that has hundreds of employees. Even if you have become the leader of a group by election, it is not easy to lead the whole group. To be able to unite so many people and lead them, one must be able to gain the hearts of people through spiritual gentleness.

Of course, people may follow those who have power or those who are rich and seem to help the needy in this world. A Korean saying goes, "When a minister's dog dies there is a flood of mourners, but when the minister himself dies, there is no mourner." As in this saying, we can find out whether a person really had the quality of generosity when he loses his power and wealth. When a person is rich and powerful, people seem to follow him, but it is difficult to find anybody who stays with a person until the end even though he has lost all his power and wealth.

But he who has virtue and generosity is followed by many people even if he loses his power and wealth. They follow him not for monetary gain, but to find rest in him.

156

Even in the church, some leaders say it is hard because they are not able to accept and embrace just a handful of cell group members. If they want to have revival in their group, they should first cultivate a gentle heart that is as soft as cotton. Then, the members will find rest in their leaders, enjoying peace and happiness, so revival will automatically follow. Pastors and ministers must be very gentle and be able to accept many souls.

There are blessings given to the gentle. Matthew 5:5 says, *"Blessed are the gentle, for they shall inherit the earth."* As mentioned earlier, to inherit the earth does not mean we will receive land here in this world. It means we will receive land in Heaven to the extent that we have cultivated spiritual gentleness in our heart. We will receive a big enough house in Heaven so that we can invite every soul who found rest in us.

Getting such a big dwelling place in Heaven also means we will be in a very honorable position, too. Even if we have such a large piece of land on Earth, we cannot take it to Heaven. But the land that we receive in Heaven by cultivating a gentle heart will be our inheritance that will not disappear forever. We will enjoy eternal happiness in our place along with the Lord and our beloved ones.

Therefore, I hope you will diligently plow your heart to bear the beautiful fruit of gentleness, so that you can inherit a large piece of land as your inheritance in the heavenly kingdom like that of Moses.

1 Corinthians 9:25

"Everyone who competes in the games exercises

self-control in all things.

They then do it to receive a perishable wreath,

but we, one that is imperishable."

Chapter 10

Self-Control

Self-Control

A marathon is a 42.195 km (26 miles and 385 yards) race. The runners have to manage their pace well to get to the finish line. It is not a short distance race that ends quickly, so they must not run at full speed randomly. They have to keep a very steady pace throughout the entire course, and when they get to an appropriate point, they might give the last spurt of energy.

The same principle applies to our lives. We have to be steadily faithful until the end in our race of faith and win the struggle against ourselves to gain the victory. Furthermore, those who want to receive glorious crowns in the heavenly kingdom must be able to exercise self-control in all things.

Self-control is needed in all aspects of life

We can see in this world that those who do not have self-control make their lives complex and cause difficulties for themselves. For example, if the parents give too much love to their son only because he is the only child, it is very likely that the child will be spoiled. Also, although they know they have to manage and care for their families, those who are addicted to gambling or other forms of pleasure ruin their families because they cannot control themselves. They say, "This will be the last time. I won't do it anymore," but that 'last time' continues to take place again and again.

In the famous Chinese historical novel *Romance of Three Kingdoms,* Zhang Fei is full of affection and bravery but he is short-tempered and aggressive. Liu Bei and Guan Yu, who swear brotherhood with him, are always worried that he might make

Self-control

mistakes at any moment. Zhang Fei receives much advice, but he cannot really change his character. Eventually, he faces trouble because of his hot-temper. He beats up and scourges his subordinates who do not meet his expectations, and two men who felt they were wrongfully punished hold grudges against him, assassinate him, and surrender themselves to the enemy camp.

Likewise, those who do not control their tempers hurt the feelings of many people at home and in the workplace. It is easy for them to cause enmity between themselves and others, and thus they are not likely to lead prosperous lives. But those who are wise will put the blame on themselves and bear with others even in anger-provoking situations. Even if others make big mistakes, they control their tempers and melt the hearts of the others with words of comfort. Such acts are wise acts that will gain the hearts of many people and allow for their lives to flourish.

Self-control, basic for God's children

Most basically, we, as God's children, need self-control in order to cast away sins. The less self-control we have, the more difficulty we feel in casting away sins. When we listen to the Word of God and receive God's grace, we make up our mind to change ourselves, but we may still be tempted by the world again.

We can see this by the words that come from our lips. Many people pray to make their lips holy and perfect. But in their lives, they forget what they prayed for, and they just speak as they wish, following old habits. When they see something happen that is hard for them to understand because it goes against what they think or believe, some people soon grumble and complain about it.

They may regret it after complaining, but they cannot control themselves when their emotions are stirred. Also, some people like talking so much that they cannot stop once they start talking. They do not have discernment between words of truth and untruth, and things that they should say and should not, so they make many mistakes.

We can understand how important self-control is just by seeing this aspect of controlling our words.

Self-control perfects the fruits of the Holy Spirit

But the fruit of self-control, as in one of the fruits of the Holy Spirit, does not simply refer to controlling ourselves from committing sins. The self-control as in one of the fruits of the Holy Spirit controls other fruits of the Holy Spirit so they can become perfect. For this reason, the first fruit of the Spirit is love and the last is self-control. Self-control is relatively less noticeable than other fruits, but it is very important. It controls everything so there can be stability, organization and concreteness. It is mentioned last among other fruits of the Spirit because all the other fruits can be perfected through self-control.

For example, even though we have the fruit of joy, we cannot just express our joy anywhere any time. When other people are mourning in a funeral, if you have a big smile on your face, what might they say about you? They will not say you are gracious for you are bearing the fruit of joy. Even though the joy of receiving salvation is so great, we need to control it according to situations. This way we can make it a true fruit of the Holy Spirit.

It is important to have self-control when we are faithful to God as well. Especially, if you have many duties, you have to allocate your time appropriately so you can be where you need to be the most at the appropriate time. Even when a particular meeting is very gracious, you need to finish it when it needs to be finished. Likewise, to be faithful in all God's household, we need the fruit of self-control.

It's the same with all other fruits of the Holy Spirit, including love, mercy, goodness, etc. When the fruits that are borne in heart are shown in deeds, we have to follow the guidance and voice of the Holy Spirit to make it the most appropriate. We can prioritize the work to be done first and that which can be done later. We can determine whether we should go forward or step back. We can have this kind of discernment through this fruit of the self-control.

If somebody has borne all the fruits of the Holy Spirit completely, it means he is following the desires of the Holy Spirit in all things. In order to follow the desires of the Holy Spirit and act in perfection, we have to have the fruit of self-control. That is why we say that all the fruits of the Holy Spirit are completed through this fruit of self-control, the last fruit.

Against Such Things There Is No Law

Evidences of the fruit of self-control having been borne

When other fruits of the Holy Spirit borne in the heart are shown externally, the fruit of self-control becomes like an arbitration center that gives harmony and order. Even when we take something good in the Lord, taking all you can is not always the best. We say something in excess is worse than something deficient. In spirit, too, we have to do everything in moderation following the desires of the Holy Spirit.

Now, let me explain how the fruit of self-control can be shown in detail.

First, we will follow the order or hierarchy in all things.

By understanding our position in the order, we will understand when we should act or not and the words that we should or should not speak. Then, there won't be any disputes, quarrels, or misunderstandings. Also, we don't do anything that is inappropriate or things that go beyond the limits of our position. For example, suppose the leader of a mission group asked the administrator to do a certain work. This administrator is full of passion, and he feels that he has a better idea, so he changed some things at his discretion and did the work accordingly. Then, even though he worked with so much passion, he did not keep the order by changing things due to lack of self-control.

God can regard us highly when we follow the order according to different positions in mission groups of the church, such as the president, vice president, administrator, secretary, or treasurer. Our leaders might have different ways of doing things than our own. Then, even though our own ways look much better and are likely to yield much more fruit, we cannot bear good fruit if the order and peace is broken. Satan always intervenes when peace is broken, and God's work will be hindered. Unless a certain thing is completely untruth, we have to think of the whole group, and obey and pursue peace according to the order so that everything can be done beautifully.

Secondly, we can consider the contents, the timing, and location even when we do something good.

For example, to cry out in prayer is something good, but if you cry out at any random location without discretion, it may disgrace God. Also, when you preach the gospel or visit the members to offer spiritual guidance, you should have discernment of the words you speak. Even though you understand some deep spiritual things, you cannot just spread it to everybody. If you deliver something that does not suit the measure of faith of the listener, then it may cause that person to stumble or pass judgment and condemnation.

In some cases, a person might give his testimony or deliver what he has spiritually understood to people who are busy with other works. Even though the content is very good, he cannot really edify others unless it is delivered in an appropriate situation. Even though others might be hearing him not to be rude to him, they cannot really pay attention to the testimony for they are busy and nervous. Let me give you another example. When a whole

Against Such Things There Is No Law

parish or a group of people has a meeting with me for consultation, and if one person keeps on telling his testimonies, what would happen to that meeting? That person is giving glory to God because he is full of grace and the Spirit. But as a result, this individual is personally using up all the time that is allocated for the whole group. This is due to lack of self-control. Even though you are doing something very good, you should consider all kinds of situations and have self-control.

Thirdly, we are not impatient or in a hurry but calm so we are able to react to each situation with discernment.

Those who have no self-control are impatient and lack consideration for others. As they hurry, they have less power of discernment, and they may miss some important things. They hastily pass judgment and condemnation that causes discomfort among others. For those who are impatient when they listen to or reply to others, they make many mistakes. We should not impatiently interrupt while someone else is talking. We should listen carefully until the end so we can avoid hasty conclusions. Furthermore, this way we can understand the intention of that person and react to it accordingly.

Before he received the Holy Spirit, Peter had an impatient and outgoing character. He tried desperately to control himself before Jesus, but even so, sometimes his character was revealed. When Jesus told Peter that he would deny Him before the crucifixion, Peter immediately refuted what Jesus said, saying he would never deny the Lord.

If Peter had had the fruit of self-control, he wouldn't have just disagreed with Jesus, but he would have tried to find the correct response. Had he known that Jesus is the Son of God, and that He would never say something meaningless, he should have kept Jesus' words in his mind. By doing so, he could have been cautious enough that it would not have happened. Proper discernment that enables us to react appropriately comes from self-control.

The Jews had great pride in themselves. They were so proud that they kept the Law of God strictly. And since Jesus rebuked Pharisees and Sadducees who were the political and religious leaders, they could not have favorable feelings towards Him. Especially, when Jesus said He is the Son of God, they considered it blasphemy. At that time the Feast of Booths was near. Around the harvest time, they set up the booths to remember the Exodus and give thanks to God. People usually went up to Jerusalem to celebrate the festivity.

But Jesus was not going to Jerusalem although the Feast was near, and His brothers urged Him to go to Jerusalem, show miracles, and reveal Himself to gain the support from people (John 7:3-5). They said, *"For no one does anything in secret when he himself seeks to be known publicly."* (v.4). Even though something seems to be so reasonable, it has no relation with God unless it is in accordance with His will. Because of their own thoughts, even the brothers of Jesus thought it was not right when they saw Jesus waiting for His time quietly.

If Jesus had not had self-control, He would have gone up to Jerusalem immediately to reveal Himself. But He was not shaken by the words of His brothers. He only waited for the proper time and for the providence of God to be revealed. And then He went up to Jerusalem quietly unnoticed by the people after all the

Against Such Things There Is No Law

brothers had gone to Jerusalem. He acted by the will of God knowing exactly when to go and when to stay.

If you want to bear the fruit of self-control

When we talk with others, many times their words and inner hearts are different. Some try to reveal other people's faults in order to cover up their own faults. They may ask for something to fulfill their greed, but they ask as if it were a request for somebody else. They seem to ask a question to understand the will of God, but in fact, they are trying to draw out the answer they want. But if you calmly talk with them, we can see that their heart is eventually revealed.

Those who have self-control will not be easily shaken by other people's words. They can calmly listen to others and can discern the truth by the works of the Holy Spirit. If they discern with self-control and answer, they can reduce many mistakes that may be caused due to wrong decisions. To that extent, they will have the authority and weight to their words, so their words can have a heavier impact on others. Now, how can we bear this important fruit of self-control?

First, we must have unchanging hearts.

We have to cultivate truthful hearts that have no falsehood or cunningness. Then we can have the power to do what we decide to do. Of course, we cannot just cultivate this kind of heart overnight. We need to keep on training ourselves, beginning with

169

keeping our hearts in small things.

There were a certain master and his apprentices. One day they were passing through a market place and some of the merchants in the market had a misunderstanding about them and started an argument with them. The disciples were enraged and entered into the quarrel, but the master was calm. After they came back from the market, he took out from the closet a bundle of letters. The letters contained contents that criticized him groundlessly, and he showed them to his pupils.

Then he said, "I cannot avoid being misunderstood. But I do not care about being misunderstood by people. I cannot avoid the first filthiness that comes to me, but I can still avoid the foolishness of taking the second filthiness."

Here, the first filthiness is to become an object of gossip of other people. The second filthiness is to have uncomfortable feelings and get into arguments and quarrels because of such gossips.

If we can have a heart that is like that of this master, we will not be shaken by any kind of situation. But rather we will be able to keep our hearts, and our lives will be at peace. Those who can keep their heart can control themselves in everything. To the extent that we cast off all kinds of evil such as hatred, envy, and jealousy, we can be trusted and loved by God.

The things that my parents taught me in my childhood helped me greatly in my pastoral ministry. While I was taught about proper ways of speech, gaits, and proper manners and behaviors, I learned to keep my heart and control myself. Once we make up our minds, we have to keep it and not change it following our own benefit. As we accumulate such efforts, we will eventually

Against Such Things There Is No Law

have an unchanging heart and gain the power of self-control.

Next, we must train ourselves to listen to the desires of the Holy Spirit by not considering our own opinion first.

To the extent that we learn the Word of God, the Holy Spirit lets us hear His voice through the Word we learned. Even if we are wrongfully accused, the Holy Spirit tells us to forgive and love. Then, we can think, 'This person must have a reason for doing what he is doing. I will try to let his misunderstanding go away by reasoning with him in a friendly way.' But if our heart has more of untruths, we will first hear the voice of Satan. 'If I leave him alone, he will keep looking down on me. I must teach him a lesson.' Even if we might hear the voice of the Holy Spirit, we will miss it because it is too weak compared to the overwhelming evil thoughts.

Therefore, we can hear the voice of the Holy Spirit when we diligently cast off the untruths that are in our hearts and keep the Words of God in our hearts. We will be able to increasingly hear the Holy Spirit's voice more as we obey even the weak voice of the Spirit. We have to try to hear the voice of the Holy Spirit first, rather than what we think is more urgent and what we think is good. Then, as we hear His voice and receive His urging, we have to obey it and put it into practice. As we train ourselves to pay attention to and obey the desires of the Holy Spirit all the time, we will be able to discern even very faint voice of the Holy Spirit. Then, we will be able to have harmony in all things.

In a sense, it might seem that the self-control has the least prominent character among all the nine fruits of the Holy Spirit.

However, it is necessary in all the areas of the various fruits. It is self-control that controls all the other eight fruits of the Holy Spirit: love, joy, peace, patience, kindness, goodness, faithfulness, and gentleness. Furthermore, all the other eight fruits will be made complete only with the fruit of self-control, and for this reason the last fruit self-control is important.

Each of these fruits of the Holy Spirit is more precious and more beautiful than any of the precious gemstones of this world. We can receive everything we ask in prayer and we will prosper in all things if we bear the fruits of the Holy Spirit. We can also reveal the glory of God by manifesting the power and authority of the Light in this world. I hope you will long for and possess fruits of the Holy Spirit more than any treasure of this world.

Against Such Things There Is No Law

Galatians 5:22-23

"But the fruit of the Spirit is

Love, joy, peace, patience,

Kindness, goodness, faithfulness, gentleness, self-control;

Against such things there is no law."

Chapter 11

Against such things there is no law

For you were called to freedom
Walk by the Spirit
The first of the nine fruits is love
Against such things there is no law

Against such things there is no law

The apostle Paul was a Jew of Jews, and he was going to Damascus to arrest Christians. On his way, however, he met the Lord and repented. He did not realize the truth of the gospel in which one is saved through faith in Jesus Christ at the time, but after he received the gift of the Holy Spirit he came to lead the evangelism of the Gentiles by the guidance of the Holy Spirit.

The nine fruits of the Holy Spirit are recorded in chapter 5 of the book of Galatians, which is one of his epistles. If we understand the situations of that time, we can understand the reason why Paul wrote Galatians and how important it is for Christians to bear the fruit of the Spirit.

For you were called to freedom

In his first missionary trip Paul went to Galatia. At the synagogue, he did not preach the Law of Moses and circumcision, but only the gospel of Jesus Christ. His words were confirmed by the following signs, and many people came into salvation. The believers in the church of Galatia loved him so much that, if possible, they would have plucked out their eyes and given them to Paul.

After Paul finished his first missionary trip and returned to Antioch, a problem arose in the church. Some people came from Judea and taught that the Gentiles had to get circumcised to receive salvation. Paul and Barnabas had great dissension and debate with them.

The brethren determined that Paul and Barnabas and a few others should go up to Jerusalem to the apostles and elders concerning this issue. They felt the need to come to a conclusion about the Law of Moses while preaching the gospel to the Gentiles both in the church of Antioch and Galatia.

Acts chapter 15 depicts the situations before and after the Council of Jerusalem, and from it we can infer how serious the situation was at that time. The apostles, who were the disciples of Jesus, and elders and church representatives gathered and had heated discussions, and they concluded that the Gentiles had to abstain from things contaminated by idols and from fornication and from what is strangled and from blood.

They sent men to Antioch to deliver the official letter which wrote about the conclusion of the Council, since Antioch was the center place of evangelism of the Gentiles. They gave some freedom to the Gentiles in keeping the Law of Moses because it would be very difficult for them to keep the Law just like the Jews. This way, any Gentile could receive salvation by believing in Jesus Christ.

Acts 15:28-29 says, *"For it seemed good to the Holy Spirit and to us to lay upon you no greater burden than these essentials: that you abstain from things sacrificed to idols and from blood and from things strangled and from fornication; if you keep yourselves free from such things, you will do well. Farewell."*

The conclusion of the Council of Jerusalem was delivered to the churches, but those who did not understand the truth of the gospel and the way of the cross kept on teaching in the churches that the believers had to keep the Law of Moses. Some false prophets also entered the church and agitated the believers criticizing the apostle Paul who did not teach the Law.

When such an incident took place in the church of Galatia, Paul the apostle explained about true freedom of Christians in his letter. Saying he used to keep the Law of Moses very strictly but became an apostle for the Gentiles after meeting the Lord, he taught them the truth of the gospel saying, *"This is the only thing I want to find out from you: did you receive the Spirit by the works of the Law, or by hearing with faith? Are you so foolish? Having begun by the Spirit, are you now being perfected by the flesh? Did you suffer so many things in vain if indeed it was in vain? So then, does He who provides you with the Spirit and works miracles among you, do it by the works of the Law, or by hearing with faith?"* (Galatians 3:2-5)

He asserted that the gospel of Jesus Christ that he taught is true because it was revelation from God, and the reason why the Gentile did not have to circumcise their body was because the important thing was to circumcise their heart. He also taught them about the desires of the flesh and those of the Holy Spirit, and about the works of the flesh and the fruits of the Holy Spirit. It was to let them understand how they were supposed to use their freedom they gained by the truth of the gospel.

Walk by the Spirit

Then, what is the reason God gave the Law of Moses? It was because people were evil and they did not recognize sins as sin. God let them have an understanding about sins, and let them solve the problem of sins and reach the righteousness of God. But the problem of sins could not be completely resolved by the deeds of the Law, and for this reason, God let the people reach the righteousness of God through faith in Jesus Christ. Galatians 3:13-14 reads, *"Christ redeemed us from the curse of the Law, having become a curse for us for it is written, 'Cursed is everyone who hangs on a tree' in order that in Christ Jesus the blessing of Abraham might come to the Gentiles, so that we would receive the promise of the Spirit through faith."*

But it does not mean the Law was abolished. Jesus said in Matthew 5:17, *"Do not think that I came to abolish the Law or the Prophets; I did not come to abolish but to fulfill,"* and said in the following verse 20, *"For I say to you that unless your righteousness surpasses that of the scribes and Pharisees, you will not enter the kingdom of heaven."*

The apostle Paul said to the believers in Galatian church, *"My children, with whom I am again in labor until Christ is formed in you"* (Galatians 4:19), and in conclusion he advised them saying, *"For you were called to freedom, brethren; only do not turn your freedom into an opportunity for the flesh, but through love serve one another. For the whole Law is fulfilled in one word, in the statement 'You shall love your neighbor as yourself' But if you bite and devour one another, take care that you are not consumed by one another"* (Galatians 5:13-15).

As children of God who have received the Holy Spirit, what do we have to do in order to serve one another through love until Christ is formed in us? We have to walk by the Holy Spirit so that we will not carry out the desires of the flesh. We can love our neighbors and have the form of Christ in us if we bear the nine

Against Such Things There Is No Law

fruits of the Holy Spirit through His guidance.

Jesus Christ received the curse of the Law and died on the cross though He was innocent, and through Him we gained freedom. In order for us not to become slaves of sin again, we have to bear the fruit of the Spirit.

If we commit sins again with this freedom and crucify the Lord all over again by committing the works of the flesh, we will not inherit the kingdom of God. On the contrary, if we bear the fruit of the Spirit by walking in the Spirit, God will protect us so that the enemy devil and Satan will not harm us. Furthermore, we will receive anything we ask in prayer.

> *"Beloved, if our heart does not condemn us, we have confidence before God; and whatever we ask we receive from Him, because we keep His commandments and do the things that are pleasing in His sight. This is His commandment: believe in the name of His Son Jesus Christ, and love one another, just as He commanded us."* (1 John 3:21-23).

> *"We know that no one who is born of God sins; but He who was born of God keeps him, and the evil one does not touch him"* (1 John 5:18).

We can bear the fruit of the Spirit and enjoy true freedom as Christians when we have the faith to walk in the Spirit and the faith working through love.

Against such things there is no law

The first of the nine fruits is love

The first fruit of the nine fruits of the Spirit is love. The love as in 1 Corinthians 13 is the love to cultivate spiritual love while love as one of the fruits of the Holy Spirit is at a higher level; it is limitless and endless love, which fulfills the Law. It is the love of God and Jesus Christ. If we have this love, we can sacrifice ourselves completely by the help of the Holy Spirit.

We can bear the fruit of joy to the extent that we cultivate this love, so that we can rejoice and be glad in all kinds of circumstances. This way, we will not have any problem with anybody, so we will bear the fruit of peace.

As we maintain peace with God, with ourselves, and with everybody else, we will naturally bear the fruit of patience. The kind of patience that God wants is that we do not even have to bear with anything because we have complete goodness and truth in us. If we have true love, we can understand and accept any kind of person without having any ill-feelings. Therefore, we would not have to forgive or endure in our heart.

When we are patient with others in goodness, we will bear the fruit of kindness. If in goodness we are patient with even those people whom we cannot really understand, then we can show kindness to them. Even if they do things that are completely out of norm, we will understand their standpoints and accept them.

Those who bear the fruit of kindness will also have goodness. They will consider others better than themselves and look out for the interests of others as well as their own. They do not argue with anybody, and they would not raise their voices. They will

Against Such Things There Is No Law

have the heart of the Lord who does not cut off a bruised reed or put out a person like a smoldering wick. If you bear such fruit of goodness, you will not insist on your opinions. You will just be faithful in all God's household and be gentle.

Those who are gentle would not become a stumbling block to anybody, and they can have peace with everyone. They possess a generous heart so that they do not pass judgment or condemnation but only understand and accept others.

In order to bear the fruits of love, joy, peace, patience, kindness, goodness, faithfulness, and gentleness in harmony, there must be self-control. Abundance in God is good, but God's works must be accomplished following order. We need self-control not to overdo anything, even if it is something good. As we follow the will of the Holy Spirit this way, God causes all to work together for good.

Against such things there is no law

The Helper, the Holy Spirit, leads God's children to the truth so they can enjoy true freedom and happiness. True freedom is salvation from sins and the power of Satan who tries to stop us from serving God and enjoying a happy life. It is also happiness gained by having fellowship with God.

As recorded in Romans 8:2, *"For the law of the Spirit of life in Christ Jesus has set you free from the law of sin and of death,"* it is the freedom that can be gained only when we believe in Jesus Christ in our heart and walk in the Light. This freedom cannot be achieved by human strength. It can never be gained without the grace of God, and it is a blessing that we can enjoy continually as long as we keep our faith.

Jesus also said in John 8:32, *"...and you will know the truth, and the truth will make you free."* Freedom is the truth, and it is unchanging. It becomes life to us and it leads us to eternal life. There is no truth in this perishing and changing world; only the unchanging Word of God is the truth. To know the truth is to learn the Word of God, keep it in mind, and to put it into practice.

But it may not always be easy to practice the truth. People have the untruths that they learned before they came to know God, and such untruths hinder them from practicing the truth. The law of flesh that desires to follow the untruth and the law of the Spirit of life that desires to follow the truth will wage war against each other (Galatians 5:17). This is a war to gain the freedom of truth. This war will go on until our faith is firm and we stand on the rock of faith that is never shaken.

As we stand on the rock of faith, it feels much easier to fight the good fight. When we cast away all evil and become sanctified, that is when we will finally be able to enjoy freedom of truth. We will not have to fight the good fight any longer because we will only practice the truth all the time. If we bear the fruits of the Holy Spirit by His guidance, nobody can stop us from having the freedom of truth.

That is why Galatians 5:18 reads, *"But if you are led by the Spirit, you are not under the Law,"* and the following verses 22-23 reads, *"But the fruit of the Spirit is love, joy, peace, patience, kindness, goodness, faithfulness, gentleness, self-control; against such things there is no law."*

Against Such Things There Is No Law

The message on the nine fruits of the Holy Spirit is like the key to open the gate of blessings. But just because we have the key the door of blessings will not open itself. We have to actually put the key in the lock and open it, and the same applies to the Word of God. No matter how much we hear, it is not completely ours yet. We can receive the blessings contained in the Word of God only when we put it into practice.

Matthew 7:21 says, *"Not everyone who says to Me, 'Lord, Lord,' will enter the kingdom of heaven, but he who does the will of My Father who is in heaven will enter."* James 1:25 says, *"But one who looks intently at the perfect law, the law of liberty, and abides by it, not having become a forgetful hearer but an effectual doer, this man will be blessed in what he does."*

In order for us to receive God's love and blessings, it is important to understand what the fruits of the Holy Spirit are, keep them in our minds, and actually bear those fruits by practicing the Word of God. If we bear the fruits of the Holy Spirit completely by practicing the truth completely, we will enjoy true freedom in the truth. We will clearly hear the voice of the Holy Spirit and be guided in all our ways, so that we will prosper in all respects. I pray in the name of the Lord that you will enjoy great honor both on this earth and in New Jerusalem, our final destination of faith.

Against such things there is no law

The Author:
Dr. Jaerock Lee

Dr. Jaerock Lee was born in Muan, Jeonnam Province, Republic of Korea, in 1943. While in his twenties, Dr. Lee suffered from a variety of incurable diseases for seven years and awaited death with no hope for recovery. However one day in the spring of 1974 he was led to a church by his sister and when he knelt down to pray, the living God immediately healed him of all his diseases.

From the moment he met the living God through that wonderful experience, Dr. Lee has loved God with all his heart and sincerity, and in 1978 he was called to be a servant of God. He prayed fervently with countless fasting prayers so that he could clearly understand the will of God, wholly accomplish it and obey the Word of God. In 1982, he founded Manmin Central Church in Seoul, Korea, and countless works of God, including miraculous healings, signs and wonders, have been taking place at his church ever since.

In 1986, Dr. Lee was ordained as a pastor at the Annual Assembly of Jesus' Sungkyul Church of Korea, and four years later in 1990, his sermons began to be broadcast in Australia, Russia, and the Philippines. Within a short time many more countries were being reached through the Far East Broadcasting Company, the Asia Broadcast Station, and the Washington Christian Radio System.

Three years later, in 1993, Manmin Central Church was selected as one of the "World's Top 50 Churches" by the Christian World magazine (US) and he received an Honorary Doctorate of Divinity from Christian Faith College, Florida, USA, and in 1996 he received his Ph. D. in Ministry from Kingsway Theological Seminary, Iowa, USA.

Since 1993, Dr. Lee has been spearheading world evangelization through many overseas crusades in Tanzania, Argentina, L.A., Baltimore City, Hawaii, and New York City of the USA, Uganda, Japan, Pakistan, Kenya, the Philippines, Honduras, India, Russia, Germany, Peru, Democratic Republic of the Congo, Israel and Estonia.

In 2002 he was acknowledged as a "worldwide revivalist" for his powerful ministries in various overseas crusades by major Christian newspapers in Korea. In particular was his 'New York Crusade 2006' held in Madison Square Garden, the most famous arena in the world. The event was broadcast to 220 nations, and in his 'Israel United Crusade 2009', held at the International Convention Center (ICC) in Jerusalem he boldly proclaimed Jesus Christ is the Messiah and Savior.

His sermons are broadcast to 176 nations via satellites including GCN TV and he was listed as one of the 'Top 10 Most Influential Christian Leaders' of 2009 and 2010 by the popular Russian Christian magazine *In Victory* and news agency Christian Telegraph for his powerful TV broadcasting ministry and overseas church-pastoring ministry.

As of October of 2013, Manmin Central Church has a congregation of more than 120,000 members. There are 10,000 branch churches world-wide including 56 domestic branch churches, and more than 123 missionaries have been commissioned to 23 countries, including the United States, Russia, Germany, Canada, Japan, China, France, India, Kenya, and many more so far.

As of the date of this publishing, Dr. Lee has written 88 books, including bestsellers *Tasting Eternal Life before Death, My Life My Faith I & II, The Message of the Cross, The Measure of Faith, Heaven I & II, Hell, Awaken Israel!,* and *The Power of God.* His works have been translated into more than 76 languages.

His Christian columns appear on *The Hankook Ilbo, The JoongAng Daily, The Chosun Ilbo, The Dong-A Ilbo, The Munhwa Ilbo, The Seoul Shinmun, The Kyunghyang Shinmun, The Korea Economic Daily, The Korea Herald, The Shisa News,* and *The Christian Press.*

Dr. Lee is currently leader of many missionary organizations and associations. Positions include: Chairman, The United Holiness Church of Jesus Christ; President, Manmin World Mission; Permanent President, The World Christianity Revival Mission Association; Founder & Board Chairman, Global Christian Network (GCN); Founder & Board Chairman, World Christian Doctors Network (WCDN); and Founder & Board Chairman, Manmin International Seminary (MIS).

Heaven I & II

A detailed sketch of the gorgeous living environment the heavenly citizens enjoy and beautiful description of different levels of heavenly kingdoms.

The Message of the Cross

A powerful awakening message for all the people who are spiritually asleep! In this book you will find the reason Jesus is the only Savior and the true love of God.

Hell

An earnest message to all mankind from God, who wishes not even one soul to fall into the depths of hell! You will discover the never-before-revealed account of the cruel reality of the Lower Grave and Hell.

My Life My Faith I & II

Dr. Jaerock Lee's autobiography provides the most fragrant spiritual aroma for the readers, through his life extracted from the love of God blossomed in midst of the dark waves, cold yoke and the deepest despair.

The Measure of Faith

What kind of a dwelling place, crown and reward are prepared for you in heaven? This book provides with wisdom and guidance for you to measure your faith and cultivate the best and most mature faith.

Spirit, Soul, and Body I & II

A guidebook that gives the reader spiritual understanding of spirit, soul, and body, and helps him find what kind of 'self' he has made so that he can gain the power to defeat darkness and become a person of spirit.

Awaken, Israel

Why has God kept His eyes on Israel from the beginning of the world to this day? What kind of His providence has been prepared for Israel in the last days, who await the Messiah?

Seven Churches

The letter to the seven churches of the Lord in the book of Revelation is for all the churches that have existed up until now. It is like a signpost for them and a summary of all the words of God in both Old and New Testaments.

Footsteps of the Lord I & II

An unraveled account of secrets about the beginning of time, the origin of Jesus, and God's providence and love for allowing His only begotten Son Passion and resurrection!

The Power of God

A must-read that serves as an essential guide by which one can possess true faith and experience the wondrous power of God

CPSIA information can be obtained
at www.ICGtesting.com
Printed in the USA
LVHW01s2354060618
579916LV00010B/231/P

9 788975 578595